Resilience of Cloud Computing in Critical Systems

Resilience, dependability, reliability in the use of

Cloud Computing

Resilience of Cloud Computing in
Critical Systems

Resilience of Cloud Computing in Critical Systems

ISBN-13: 978-1492912057

ISBN-10: 1492912050

2014 Eyeworks Publishing

London. UK

[to my family...]

Abstract

With the increasing utilization of Internet services and cloud computing by most organizations (both private and public), it is clear that computing is becoming the 5th utility (along with water, electricity, telephony and gas). These technologies are used for almost all types of systems, and the number is increasing, including Critical Infrastructure systems. Even if Critical Infrastructure systems appear not to rely directly on cloud services, there may be hidden inter-dependencies. This is true even for private cloud computing, which seems more secure and reliable. The critical systems can began in some cases with a clear and simple design, but evolved as described by Egan to "rafted" networks. Because they are usually controlled by one or few organizations, even when they are complex systems, their dependencies can be understood. The organization oversees and manages changes. These CI systems have been affected by the introduction of new ICT models like global communications, PCs and the Internet. Even virtualization took more time to be adopted by Critical systems, due to their strategic nature, but once that these technologies have been proven in other areas, at the end they are adopted as well, for different reasons such as costs. A new technology model is happening now based on some previous technologies (virtualization, distributing and utility computing, web and software services) that are offered in new ways and is called cloud computing.

The organizations are migrating more services to the cloud; this will have impact in their internal complexity and in the reliability of the systems they are offering to the organization itself and their clients. Not always this added complexity and associated risks to their reliability are seen. As well, when two or more CI systems are interacting, the risks of one can affect the rest, sharing the risks.

This work investigates the use of cloud computing by critical systems, and is focused in the dependencies and reliability of these systems. Some examples are presented together with the associated risks. A framework is introduced for analysing the dependability and resilience of a system that relies on cloud services and how to improve them. As part of the framework, the concepts of micro and macro dependability are introduced to explain the internal and external dependability on services supplied by an external cloud. A pharmacovigilance model system has been used for framework testing.

"Every Problem in computer science can be solved with another level of indirection, but this typically involves another problem"

[David Wheeler]

1   Introduction

Virtualization and Cloud computing have changed the way organizations are using ICT services. Cloud services are starting to be used for almost all types of organizations including the ones that are involved in CI (Critical Infrastructure) systems. As with virtualization in the past, cloud services have been introduced by stages, usually starting with services that are not part of critical systems. There is a long list of reasons for using the cloud model such as elasticity, mobility, costs and the possibility for the organization of focusing on the core business and use ICT as the 5th Utility. The main risk with the use of these services is not what we see, but what we do not see. As the complexity increases, new variables are introduced, in most cases without the knowledge of the organization. Egan (Egan 2007) uses the term "rafted networks" to describe this type of systems that began with simple systems which evolve into very complex systems in an unplanned manner.

The utilization of cloud computing is changing the current ICT models for most of the industries and organizations, including the public ones, impacting on the current systems, the reliability and the risks associated to these new models. It is considered that in the next years and due to the number of systems both private and public, cloud computing facilities could become a critical infrastructure, and similar protection to other critical infrastructure systems should be implemented. It should be considered also the interdependencies for these systems, and assessed the impact of possible cascade effects. This work exposes these risks, the effects on the resilience, reliability and possible solutions for improving the visibility of the risks and how to increase them.

Some examples of the use of cloud computing by critical systems are presented, as well as some of the risks related to the reliability and resilience of these systems. In the next sections, an overview of current proposals to measure and increase the reliability, dependability and resilience is presented. In the final sections, a model to represent the dependencies of these systems is described; the framework is based in the concepts of macro and micro dependability that are explained. These concepts and framework do not pretend to replace previous ones like the "coupling and hidden interactions" defined by Perrow (Perrow 1999), but complement them, so both could be applied. As well, an example is used to illustrate the use of this model and possible implementation in case of being used by organizations. No distinction is done between the different type of cloud models and architectures, but most of the times we shall use as examples "Infrastructure as a Service" model, and the Private/Community cloud for micro dependability, and Public/Community for Macro Dependability. The cloud model cepts are not described here as this is not the focus of this work and there is supplementary information in other publications such as "A view of cloud computing" (M, et al. 2010) or the Security Guidance from the Cloud Security Alliance CSA (CSA 2009).

In order to test the model, a real example has been used. For this, a typical pharmacovigilance system has been chosen. The main focus of the work will be find out what are the consequences and the risks of using cloud services on this kind of systems.

In order to create the framework there will be necessary to:

- Study the main dependability and resilience existing models, specifically the ones based on UML, like the ones defined by Bondavalli and Majzik (A. Bondavalli 1999) or the Framework sysML (Linhares, et al. 2007), and adapt them for using together with the concepts of Macro and Micro dependability.
- Use an existing framework for SLAs like the Web Service Level Agreement WSLA from Keller (Alexander Keller 2002) and Patel (P. Patel 2009), or the new WS-Agreement proposed by the GRAAP Working Group (Andrieux, et al. 2007) in the Open Grid Forum and adjust to be used with the proposed Framework in a way that some of the variables of the model like reliability could be measured and reused into the framework. This will imply the selection of a method for the calculation of the values of the variables; focusing mostly in the reliability in the same way as is calculated by Dhillon (Dhillon 2003).
- Once the framework is prepared, it will be tested with a critical health system, this will be done with a pharmacovigilance system applied as defined by Mann (Mann and Andrews 2007) in order to view how the model could be used.

1.1   Structure of the book

This chapter introduces the work of the thesis and explains the structure and content of the different chapters, as well as explaining the contribution of the work. Chapter two is dedicated to the definition of the problem; some examples of the use of cloud computing for critical services are described, as well as some cloud computing errors from different cloud vendors. In the last part of chapter two we explain the problem with the resilience of critical systems using cloud services.

Chapter three takes a look into the state of the art of dependability and resilience, with more detail into reliability in critical systems. More information related to this has been added in Appendix A.

Once the problem has been explained, Chapter four describes the proposed solution and the proposed Framework for dealing with resilience and dependability issues in cloud services. The concepts of Macro and micro dependability, as well as the concepts that are the basis of the framework are explained, and the different metrics used in the framework.

In chapter five a pharmacovigilance case is used as an example for the proposed framework, some concepts of a pharmacovigilance application are used and some proposed implementations are explained together with their benefits. The last Chapter explains the conclusions of the work and the future direction.

Appendix A includes all the main concepts of cloud computing such as standards, main vendors and toolkit. This appendix contains also a section dedicated to the current state of the government use of cloud computing and other that talks about the use of big data by public organizations and the main implications of this use.

Appendix B explains the resilience, dependability and reliability issues in cloud computing services. It explains how different cloud models and implementation could affect the dependability and reliability of the final system.

Appendix C describes the structure of an standard pharmacovigilance system that could help to understand the domain of the system tested.

1.2   Contributions of the book

This book proposes a framework for monitoring and improve resilience in critical systems based on cloud computing. The following contributions are done:

- Theoretical point of view: Creation and definition of the macro and micro dependability concepts. Definition of a new Framework for evaluation of the interdependency between systems from the resilience and reliability point of view in the area of cloud computing services.
- Methodology point of view: Define a strategy that permits the evaluation of dependability in these cloud computing systems by the possible customers of critical systems and their experience which can be used as feedback by other clients.
- Practical point of view: make an empirical assessment of the model for a critical pharmacovigilance health system, and review the possible results.

"Simplicity is a great virtue but it requires hard work to achieve it and education to appreciate it. And to make matters worse: complexity sells better."

[Edsger Dijkstra]

2   Definition of the Problem

2.1   Introduction

It could be said that currently there is not a problem with the use of Cloud computing by critical systems, mainly because it is not used, or as is presented in this work, it is not recognized. As described previously, the utilization of cloud computer as a new utility, where we can use it in the same way we use electricity or water is extended mainly for small organizations where ICT departments are too expensive to maintain. However we do not even conceive the idea of a nuclear plant, a medical device, a health service or a telephone provider using cloud services for the critical part of their infrastructure. As an example, a few years ago the same was thought from the virtualization technologies due to the added complexity, and now is widely use in some of those systems.

We could consider that this problem is not happening now, but it could happen soon; and that the criticality of the systems using these types of services could grow in the next future. This means that these new models should be taken into consideration and the possible impact in these types of systems. One issue is how we keep the same quality attributes when we add cloud services into the complexity of the system.

Another issue is that over the time more and more organizations will use these cloud services and the intrinsic criticality of these services will increase. Consequently, cloud providers and services will become a critical infrastructure too. There is a hidden risk for the organizations, mainly because there is no real control of what systems could be affected in case of cloud services failure. There are not clear interdependencies between cloud services and organization. Furthermore it is not easy to reuse one of the existing models implemented in other engineering areas because of the complexity of the system and the lack of data due to the secrecy of the cloud providers.

There are questions that arise from the use of cloud systems by organizations that provide critical services. How is possible to assess the dependability, resilience and reliability of cloud systems where these are used by our organizations? How to assure that the availability figures will match the agreement with the cloud provider SLA? What will be the impact in our systems if one of the cloud provider's services fails?

2.2   Relevance of the Problem

Cloud computing services, referred to Infrastructure as a Service (IaaS), Platform as a Service (PaaS), and Software as a Service (SaaS) delivers to consumers infrastructure, platform and software that are made available as subscription-based services in a pay-as-you-go model to consumers. These services are described by Armbrust (M, et al. 2010) as 'Cloud computing, the long-held dream of computing as a utility has the potential to transform a large part of the IT industry, making software even more attractive as a service'.

The terms dependability, reliability and resilience are used in this work. Until now, the main focus in the industry has been related to dependability of systems and its different characteristics like reliability and availability. I will use dependability and some of its characteristics as reliability, mainly because still are very important for a system and are useful when studying the resilience. In this work I will use the term resilience as well as a characteristic of the systems using cloud vendors. In this context, and according to Bouchon (Bouchon 2006) resilience is the potential to remain in a particular configuration and to maintain its feedback and functions, involving the ability of the system to reorganize following disturbance-driven changes. Other possible definition of a resilient system is one that can withstand a number of sub-system and components failures while continuing to operate normal. This is normally achieved by adding redundancy, eliminating single points of failure during the design and proper maintenance.

Usually, and especially in engineering (Gary Marshall 2002) reliability is measured in terms of the Mean Time To Failure (MTTF). The MTTF is quoted in hours and is the average time taken for each individual member of a large population of standard production parts to fail. Reliability is difficult and time consuming to measure; it is a statistical number derived from a combination of historic experience with similar components and relatively short-term tests on large numbers of the components in question. As products mature, longer-term data accumulates and confidence in the MTTF figure increases.

According to Sun et al. (Sun, et al. 2010) dependability is "a very important property for a cloud system, as it provides services with the features of high availability, high stability, high fault tolerance and dynamical extensibility". It explains as well how dependability is even more important in these types of systems due to the distributed scale of this paradigm, and at the same time more difficult to achieve. The focus for calculating the dependability is on five basic attributes of the systems property vector A for cloud systems: reliability, availability, safety, integrity and maintainability. Reliability is expressed by probability of the system performing its required function under given conditions for a stated time interval.

Other important factor from infrastructure systems included cloud systems is resilience. Kroger and Zio (Kröger and Zio 2011) define it as the ability of the systems to anticipate, cope with/absorb, resist and recover from the impact of a hazard (technical) or disaster (social). Garlick (Garlick 2011) describes how community cloud computing systems could be used instead of other types of systems (including other types of cloud) to improve resilience of the systems, especially in case of disaster where the geographic distribution of community cloud systems is higher than for traditional systems.

However, historically, reliability has been the main concern for analysing that kind of systems. There are many reliability models for computing systems, adapted to different situations and environments. There are different ways of approaching the issues of dependability and reliability in cloud environments, like modelling and simulation techniques. Modelling techniques with a strong mathematical foundation, such as Stochastic Petri Nets or Reliability Block Diagrams can be used in order to evaluate dependability for cloud computing as well. The current models used for reliability and dependability of cloud systems are based on standard reliability and dependability models used in computing systems. Traditionally there are reliability models for distributed computer systems and grid computer systems that could be used for cloud computing.

From the distributed computer systems, Pierre & Hoan (Pierre 1990) define a two level hierarchical structure where the first level is the backbone or communication sub network and the second level are nodes or terminals. The distributed program reliability in a distributed computing system is the probability of successful execution of a program running on multiple processing elements and needs to retrieve data files from other processing elements. The model takes into account all the programs that run in the different nodes. There are tools based on this concept using Minimal File Spanning Trees (MFST), like the analytical one presented by Kumar et al (V. H. Kumar 1986) and that are used in homogenously distributed hardware/software systems, and later proposed a faster algorithm for reliability evaluation.

Kumar & Agrawal (A. a. Kumar 1996) introduced "Distributed Program/System Performance Index" which can be used to compare networks with different features for application execution. As well, other concepts like the Analytical Hierarchy Process (AHP) have been used for the evaluation in distributed computing environments like the one presented by Fahmy (Fahmy 2001) based on the Markov reward models. Yeh (Yeh 2003) has extended the distributed systems reliability using a multi-state concept.

Foster et al. (Foster 2002) described the basic concepts of the grid and presented a development tool that later developed toward and Open Grid Services Architecture. The reliability needs to be calculated in the resource management system, the network, software and resources. For the resource management system Markov modelling is normally used.

Malek (Malek 2008) explains how the classical reliability assessments approaches are mainly suitable during the design stage for comparative analysis of different design options, but not for online assessment and short-term prediction, proposing runtime monitoring for deal with dynamic systems. As well it is more difficult to forecast the actual system runtime behaviour during the design and development phase. Nevertheless, the models used for distributed computer systems are not always valid for cloud environments. The main problem is that these models are based on processes running on distributed nodes in order to share the computing functions among the hosts; in most of the cases there are homogeneous distributed systems or centralized heterogeneous distributed systems (Dai 2003). These models could apply to the internal functioning of most cloud technologies, what is described later as micro-dependability, but not in more complex cloud scenarios due to the complexity of the systems and different types of interaction between providers and consumers.

Another type of models for reliability in computer systems is the one for grid computer systems. In this case and in a similar way to cloud computing, there is a large-scale resource sharing and wide-area program communication. As with cloud systems, it is difficult to analyze the grid reliability due to its highly heterogeneous and wide-area distributed characteristics. Foster et al. (Foster 2002) described the basic concepts of the grid and presented a development tool that later developed toward and Open Grid Services Architecture. Cao (Cao 2002) presented a grid computer agent-based resource management system that uses quantitative data regarding the performance of complex applications running on a local grid resource. Xie and Poh (Poh 2004) define Grid program reliability as the probability of successful execution of a given program running on multiple virtual nodes and exchanging information through virtual links with the remote resources.

Calheiros et al. (Calheiros 2011) proposed to use an extensible simulation toolkit (CloudSim) that enables modeling and simulation of Cloud computing systems and application provisioning environments. Gustavsson and Sta (Gustavsson and Stå hl 2010) introduce as well the concept of using cloud services for Critical Infrastructure, in particular for smart grid. They explain the issues of using very complex and dynamic systems, and the challenges of controlling them when used in Critical Infrastructures.

Other approaches are focused in the use of empiric data, mainly from monitoring, and sometimes use this data together with information from models. Xu and Wang (Wang 2008) define the cooperative monitoring for Internet Data Centers. In a similar way, Park et al. (JiSu Park 2011) use a Markov chain based monitoring service for fault tolerance in mobile cloud computing. Another similar approach is the one presented by Song Fu (Fu 2011) where a framework for autonomic anomaly detection in the cloud is defined.

In conclusion, it is clear that there is a problem of importance, namely the vulnerability of complex systems, that has been historically being considered from the reliability and dependability schools, and that can be considered as well from the resilience point of view. This problem applies in a similar way to cloud services and how these are used by critical systems.

2.3   Critical Infrastructure & Systems of Systems

The term 'Critical Infrastructure' (CI) is used by governments to describe any kind of assets that are essential for the functioning of a society and economy. Examples of critical infrastructure sectors given by the "DHS Daily Open Source Infrastructure Reports" include Energy, Healthcare, Communications and Emergency Services (Moteff and Parfomak October 2004)

They began in some cases with a clear and simple design, but evolved as described by Egan (Egan 2007) to "rafted" networks. They have expanded in an unplanned manner. Because they are usually controlled by one or a few organizations, even when they are complex systems, their dependencies can be understood. The organization oversees and manages changes. These CI systems have been affected by the introduction of new ICT models like global communications, PCs, the Internet, and even virtualization. It took more time to be adopted by Critical systems, due to their strategic nature, but once that these technologies have been proven in other areas; at the end they are introduced as part of CI also for different reasons like costs.

2.4   Use of Cloud Computing in Critical Systems

A new technology model is happening now using some previous technologies (virtualization, distributing and utility computing, web and software services) that are offered in new ways and is called Cloud Computing.

The range of applications where cloud computing is applied to is growing exponentially. Systems that now live in the cloud include e-health (EHR Software), email (Gmail, exchange, Lotus...), office packages (Google docs, Zoho...), collaboration and telephony tools (Google voice), specific software (CRM, ERP...), Operating systems (eyeOS) and servers and desktops (virtualization). It reduces the investment in ICT equipment and maintenance. It improves mobility permitting access from anywhere, flexibility, elasticity (can be expanded as needed), and as well it can reduce the complexity of ICT from the core business of the organization (permitting to the organization to concentrate on what they know how to do). ICT now is becoming in most cases a utility (as water, electricity) that does not need to live inside the company.

In the same way that many other previous new technologies (electric grid, telephony and Internet) have evolved to very large systems that are part of a critical infrastructure, we believe that for cloud computing the evolution would be similar. Unfortunately, the use of these systems could evolve in an uncontrolled manner, driven in part by reduced costs and easy provisioning, and in some cases even not driven directly by the ICT departments of the organizations. But what happens when these systems are managed entirely by an external company? Essentially you need to trust totally on the way the service is managed. This is normally done using contracts, Service Level Agreements like WSLA (P. Patel 2009) and audits, as well as continuing monitoring of the quality of service and mainly trust on the provider. For organizations providing CI systems, the use of cloud computing is related to non-critical functions that are not part of the Critical Services that offers. Sometimes the interrelations of these 'non-critical' functions are unknown in advance, and it is only when an error on the 'non-critical' part of the system affects the critical part that these interrelations are noticed.

This could affect as well any other 'non-critical' part of the system and does not seem that there is a difference if this is done using cloud computing or using an internal system. But the problem is that cloud computing services that initially appear as very good candidates due to the intrinsic characteristics of these systems (elasticity, mobility, reliability...), can have as well other characteristics/problems that are not known yet (Vouk 2008). Questions like sharing of resources with other clients, over utilization, lack of control, security implications... should be taken into account as these could affect the resilience and dependability. As stated by the European Union Committee in the report "Protecting Europe against large-scale cyber attacks" ((EUC) 2009), there is an increase complexity due to the use of outsourcing, off-shoring and cloud services in government and business systems. These systems process sensitive citizen information and support critical national infrastructure, being vulnerable to damaging cyber-attacks and in some cases use of cyber terrorism or cyber war (Lavenue 2009). In some cases where the environments are controlled, like defence or international organizations, there are initiatives in the use of Community clouds (Gerard Briscoe 2009), mainly in Infrastructure as a Service. These clouds represent an attempt to create private clouds between different similar organizations, varying in the grade of sharing between the different services offered.

But the main implications of these technologies will come in the near future; currently the organizations/governments do not migrate critical systems to cloud computing because it still very new and there still are questions not answered. But as previously happened with other technologies like virtualization, the organizations will start to use it, first for non-critical or non-production systems, and later, once they become comfortable with the new technology, will use it for all type of systems, including critical infrastructure systems (Gewndal Le Grand 2004). Sometimes these new technologies or new ways of use the technology could tend to create new uses beyond the ones intended when were created.

2.5 Examples of use of Cloud Services in critical systems and potential critical situations

Most of the examples of uses of cloud computing in critical systems are using the Software as a Service or Infrastructure as a service model. In most cases these systems are replacing 'non-critical' parts of the system. The main reasons to move to these technologies are costs and improved functionality.

2.5.1   Cloud offering for SCADA systems

Supervisory Control and Data Acquisition (SCADA) system, Distributed Control Systems (DCS), and other control systems are found in industrial sectors and critical infrastructure. These are known under the general term Industrial Control System (ICS). ICS are normally used in industries such as electrical, water, oil and gas. The reliable operation of infrastructure depends on computerized systems and SCADA. In the last years different vendors are providing solutions for integrate these systems with Web Dashboards that live in the cloud, Figure 1 Example of a SCADA cloud integrator vendor. Source DAQConnect shows an example from an specific vendor. The information of collected by these devices can be viewed and controlled from different types of devices from different locations. An example of an issue with SCADA systems has been the problem with the Stuxnet virus. This is the first discovered worm that spies on and reprograms industrial systems. It was specifically written to attack Supervisory Control And Data Acquisition (SCADA) systems used to control and monitor industrial processes. This particular virus is not related to cloud systems, but what will be the effect of a virus like this in a service similar to the previous example offered by a cloud provider where the services are used by multiple tenants?

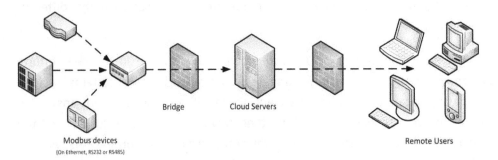

Figure 1 Example of a SCADA cloud integrator vendor. Source DAQConnect

2.5.2   Department of Defense Rapid Access computing environment (RACE)

The pentagon cybersecurity Robert Lentz (Lentz 2009)presented the benefits of private cloud computing for DoD. To meet this, the Defense Information Systems Agency (DISA) is trying a DoD-managed cloud computing environment called RACE, which enables DoD users to access virtual services and storage from a Web portal. DISA currently manages the IT infrastructure for 4 million DoD users and operates 14 data centres over the world.

The RACE portal defines this system as: "This quick-turn computing solution uses the revolutionary technology of cloud computing to give you the platform that you need today, quickly, inexpensively and, most importantly, securely." Currently the system as described by the DoD is not used for Critical functions of the DoD, but more for new test systems (i.e. YouTube for troops and families) , but this could change soon due to the success of the system.

2.5.3   Critical Government services in Peru

IBM and FONAFE (Fondo Nacional de Financiamiento de la Actividad Empresarial del Estado) are working on the creation of a private cloud infra-structure for centralizing the IT operations of 10 government companies that provide critical services like transportation, power utility, postal, port ship-ping in Peru. This will include the consolidation of 10 Datacenters, using an outsourced model based on private cloud. The purpose is to reduce costs and improve efficiency.

2.5.4   Air Transport Industry (ATI) Cloud

This is a global cloud infrastructure offering on-demand services to the airline industry by Orange and SITA. The cloud computing infrastructure, named as the Air Transport Industry (ATI) Cloud, use six data centres in Sydney, Hong Kong, Singapore, Johannesburg, Frankfurt and Atlanta.

Each data centre will primarily cover their own regions and will be interconnected via high-speed MPLS (multi-protocol label switching) network. ATI will offer their portfolio of services, encompassing including infrastructure-as-a-service (IaaS), platform-as-a-service (PaaS), desktop-as-a-service (DaaS), and software-as-a-service (SaaS). According to the studies by SITA, 93% of airlines plan to implement cloud computing services by 2014.

Created and owned by the air transport community it serves, SITA's reservations system boards 100 million plus passengers a year, and is used by over 165 airlines worldwide.

2.5.5   Radio system for emergency services (SaaS)

The purpose of this system is to allow the fire brigade, police, emergency management and other type of public agencies to connect their private push-to-talk radio systems to others inside their agency and connect as well with other agencies that has been authorized previously. These tasks are not executed in their local servers and instead are moved into shared datacentres accessed via the Internet.

There are several benefits described by these companies on the use of these infrastructures, for these agencies, most of them related to the use of Cloud systems. The main benefits are the low entry barriers of cost for using these technologies, as there is no need of big investment on interoperability infrastructure, as this is changed for a pay-per-use model.

2.5.6   Nasa Nebula IaaS

Nebula is an open-source cloud computing project and service created by NASA (Shackelford 2011). It was developed to provide an alternative to the costly construction of additional data centers used by NASA scientists or engineers require additional data processing. Nebula as well provides a simplified way for NASA scientists and researchers to share large, complex data sets with external partners and the public. The model is based on the open standard "OpenStack" for open source cloud computer that follows a similar model to Linux, and is based on two key components, OpenStack Compute that is software to provision and manage large groups of virtual servers, and OpenStack Object Storage, for creating redundant, scalable object storage using clusters of commodity servers to store large quantities of data.

2.5.7   Electronic Health Record

The electronic health records are becoming more used, and the cloud is becoming a very cheap way to maintain this information. Many citizens and organizations are using systems like Google Health for keeping historic clinic records. The risks of these services are not only the data protection related, but the quality of the data, that could induce medical errors like a cancer spreading into the brain and spine because of data improperly imported.

2.5.8   New initiatives

There still appearing more new initiatives of using cloud services for Critical systems, one example is Google Crisis Response. Has been used for all types of disasters like the earthquake in Christchurch (New Zealand), the Fukushima's disaster, or the Irene Hurricane in 2011.

2.6   Cloud computing errors

Here are presented some errors happened in different cloud computing systems. New errors are appearing at least every month from one of the big cloud providers. These are just a few included as example of what types of errors.

2.6.1   Amazon cloud outages

2.6.1.1   *April 2011 EC2 outage in Virginia Datacenter*

Affected for several days the west coast datacentre of Amazon, affecting several companies with intermittent unavailability. Part of the Elastic block storage was unavailable and was not possible to read data. This was due to a network upgrade. There was a human error that routed the traffic to a network path with less bandwidth, leading to saturation in the network. All the replicas of the servers were not available anymore and automatically new replicas started to be created, what is known as a "replica storm". Soon, there were not resources anymore. In order to solve the problem more resources until the problem was solved by itself, just to avoid restarting all these servers and affecting even more to customers.

2.6.1.2   *Elevated levels of authenticated requests from multiple users 2006*

The request volumes are monitored, but the cryptographic overhead was not considered. It occurred an overload on the authentication services that perform the request processing and validation. The S3 service that is used for the cloud storage became inaccessible, and this is the only storage facility supported by amazon hosted virtual servers. It took 3 hours to solve it.

2.6.1.3   *Outage from bitbucket.org 2009*

IT was a UDP /TCP flooding attack that was not successful, but this influenced also the access to the storage facility.

2.6.1.4   *Others*

2008 Single-bit error in transmitted system state lead to global S3 storage outage, took 6 hours to repair, including complete reboot.

2011 Outage of S3, Web 2.0 companies affected for days

This is the email Amazon sent to a big customer letting them know that some of their data was gone.

> *Hello,*
>
> *A few days ago we sent you an email letting you know that we were working on recovering an inconsistent data snapshot of one or more of your Amazon EBS volumes. We are very sorry, but ultimately our efforts to manually recover your volume were unsuccessful. The hardware failed in such a way that we could not forensically restore the data.*
>
> *What we were able to recover has been made available via a snapshot, although the data is in such a state that it may have little to no utility...*

If you have no need for this snapshot, please delete it to avoid incurring storage charges.

We apologize for this volume loss and any impact to your business.

Sincerely,

Amazon Web Services, EBS Support

2.6.2   Microsoft cloud outages

2.6.2.1   *September 2011 DNS issue*

Microsoft originally blogged that the downtime was due to a southern California power outage, but this post was quickly removed from the site. Later, Microsoft said that the preliminary root cause was a DNS issue and that they were working diligently to restore service. Microsoft Outages cloud-based services (Office 365, Skydrive, Hotmail) Sept 2011 - Preliminary root cause suggests a DNS issue

2.6.2.2   *Microsoft Exchange Online May 2011*

Affected the Microsoft Business Productivity Online Suite (BPOS), that is used by companies to support their mail, SharePoint and office suite requirements. The issue affected during two weeks of with mainly email glitches.

2.6.2.3   *Others*

2009 T-Mobile Sidekick, one week data outage, permanent data loss for customers

2.6.3   Vmware cloud outages

2.6.3.1   *April 2011 VMware CloudFoundry*

All started with an intermittent failure in two of the DEA (executing) nodes; this is usually a normal event. The failure started to spread over nodes, affecting the scheduler. After half an hour, the nodes were stabilized, but all redundant cloud controllers lost the connectivity to the storage system. Due to not having storage force to go to read only mode, creating a problem to the client computers. IT was identified that the main cause was the lost of a LUN to the storage. It seems that the cloud controller could not manage properly the partial lost of connectivity to the LUN. The event took hours to be solved. VMWare declared that this was a combination of misaligned software, procedures and monitoring system. They tried to avoid this to happened again, and they created a full operation playbook related to this error, and during this creation of this one of the engineers execute this by mistake in production and bring down the front-end of the network infrastructure and all the CloudFoundry platform was not reachable externally, taking 1 hour and 15 minutes to have the system up again.

2.7   Problem: Resilience and Reliability in Critical Systems using cloud services

We have seen that some systems that could be used for critical situations rely on cloud services. But mainly cloud services are created for providing standard services; services that are cheap due to the economies of scale, and usually the resilience or reliability are not always the main drivers of these services, but the costs. This does not mean that the resilience or reliability are not good, as normally are.

The requirement for resilience and reliability depend of the system that is supported. As an example, in the transatlantic cable service, the amplifiers used underwater must operate for 20 years without failure, just because the cost of raising and repairing the cable alone would be more than £500 000, and the total cost including the loss of revenue during the repair will be more than one million pounds (G. Dummer 1997).

So this work will focus on the resilience and reliability when using cloud services, especially for systems that could be considered critical. Reliability is a very important factor for the correct functioning of these systems, especially on the safety of the system, but as described by Nancy Leveson (technology 2001) in the software safety myths, it is not the only one, and not always increasing software reliability will increase safety. This is why others factors like maintainability, costs and others will be mentioned and in some cases covered in detail. A system can perform perfectly and in a reliable way its required function and at the same time be unsafe.

The problem to be addressed in this book can be stated as follows:

The models that we have been using in different areas in the last 40 years are not more valid for the complexity of the new ICT models, and in particular cloud computing. It is not feasible to try to understand all the combinations of possible mishaps. Assess them is a challenge due to the dynamicity and changes of the systems, the increasing complexity and the growing connectivity and interoperability. We need to find new models and frameworks to address resilience in very complex cloud environments, trying to probe the dependability without knowing all the details of the system and without having a complete model.

A framework will be proposed in this Book that will help an organization to study the dependability characteristics of using a cloud service, focusing mainly in the resilience of the complete system, using empiric data gathered from monitoring systems, not only provided by that vendor but from other parties as well.

"Simplicity is prerequisite for reliability."

[E. Dijkstra]

3 Resilience, Dependability, Reliability and Cloud Computer

3.1 Introduction

In this section, the main concepts related to cloud systems and critical infrastructure will be covered, and the main terminology will be introduced.

3.2 Resilience

The term resilience is used to define the ability of a system to provide and maintain an acceptable service level when challenges occur during the normal operation. Laprie (Laprie and LAAS-CNRS n.d.) define resilience as the persistence of service delivery that can justifiably be trusted, when facing changes like unexpected failures, attacks, accidents or increased load. According to Bouchon (Bouchon 2006) resilience is the potential to remain in a particular configuration and to maintain its feedback and functions, involving the ability of the system to reorganize following disturbance-driven changes.

Other possible definition of a resilient system is one that can withstand a number of sub-system and components failures while continuing to operate normal. This is normally achieved by adding redundancy, eliminating single points of failure during the design and proper maintenance. Kishor et al (Trivedi, Kim and Ghosh 2009) give more details about the definitions and possible uses of Resilience in Computer Industry, as well about a comparison with dependability metrics such as availability, performance and survivability.

In order to study the resilience of a system attributes like dependability and reliability of a system should be studied. Laprie (Laprie and LAAS-CNRS n.d.) defines the term resilience as the persistence of Dependability when facing changes.

3.3 Dependability

Dependability is used to define some operational requirements on a system. It has been defined by:

- Jean-Claude Laprie: "Trustworthiness of a computer system such that reliance can be placed on the service it delivers to the user" (Avizienis, et al. 2004)
- IFIP 10.4 Working Group on Dependable Computing and Fault Tolerance as "*[..] the trustworthiness of a computing system which allows reliance to be justifiably placed on the service it delivers [..]*". (IFIP WG10.4 on Dependable computing and Fault Tolerance n.d.)
- IEC IEV 191-02-03: "*dependability (is) the collective term used to describe the availability performance and its influencing factors: reliability performance, maintainability performance and maintenance support performance*" (IEC n.d.)

Usually dependability is applied to all computer systems as part of the system quality, but this is even more important on critical systems, where in some cases can harm humans (medical devices, Aerospatiale industry, etc.). It adds a third dimension to system quality, on top of the most common cost and performance.

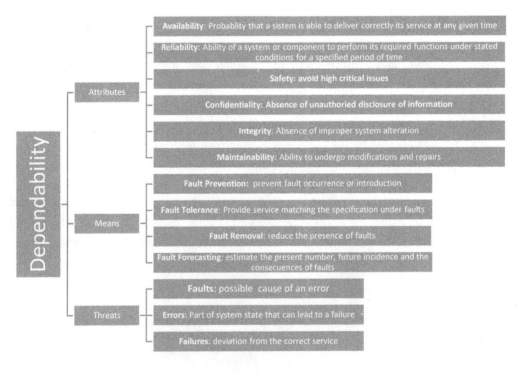

Figure 2 Dependability tree [Laprie]

Some of the reasons to build dependable systems are money (if the systems fails we will lose money), lifesaving (if the system fails people could be harm), human users (tolerate human errors), complexity, and harsh environments.

Dependability is a very broad term that is associated with a lot of different attributes as can be seen in the definition from Laprie in Figure 2 Dependability tree [Laprie]; in this work, the focus will be reliability that is one of the characteristics of a dependable system.

For the dependability means, there are two mainly techniques to treat the faults/failures. One is the fault intolerance that is used to avoid having faults, and includes fault prevention (that can be achieved by shielding, reusing of reliable components, specialized development and manufacturing process to prevent design faults, specialized specification formalisms, and the use of proper engineering approaches like quality management and training) and fault removal (done by dynamic and static verification, diagnosis and correction).

The other is fault tolerance techniques that include fault forecasting and fault tolerance, and implies that faults will appear and is focus on how we will anticipate that will happen and how the system will operate correctly in presence of faults, usually done with the use of redundancy in time (as example retrying the execution) or space (failing over, replication).

Figure 3 Chain of dependability threats [Avizienis]

Other important concept is the chain of dependability threats. Figure 11 defines the chain dependability threat from Avizienis (Avizienis, et al. 2004), where there is a fault that is in the system and must be activated before an error is generated. When the fault is activated the error estate is reached, and this can lead to a propagation of errors that can lead to a system or component failure.

3.3.1   Dependability Models

There are several models for the dependability of a system; in computer science normally formalism is used to model the system dependability. The system is described a set of components, for each component the availability is calculated, and with the system analysis of the model the availability of the system is calculated.

For the system analysis the main approaches are:

- Deductive methods (top-down), based on a system failure, try to find out what issues or components behaviors can contribute to this failure. Main examples are Fault tree analysis (FTA) or Reliability Block Diagrams (RBD)

- Inductive methods (bottom-up), checking what are the reliability events that can happen and how this evolves to system level to get a general conclusion for the system. Main examples are event trees, Preliminary Hazards Analysis (PHA), or Failure Mode and Effect Analysis (FMEA).

Main types of dependability models:

- Component based models
  - o Reliability block diagram

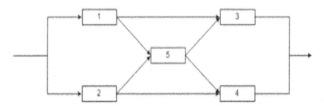

  - o Fault tree: is an application of deductive logic to produce a failure-oriented analysis, where complex system failures are broken down into simpler subsystem, components, block and single element failures.

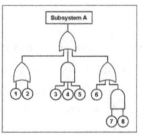

- State based models

o   Petri net: represented as a directed bipartite graph, where the nodes represent the transitions and places. The places can have a number of tokens that are distributed over the places (marking). The transition starts whenever there is a token at the start of all input arcs, when it starts; it uses these tokens, and moves tokens to the end of all output arrows. The arrows represent which places are pre and post conditions for which transitions. The execution is nondeterministic, being good technique for representing concurrent behavior of distributed systems. The good thing about petri nets compared to other model representation for distributed systems is that petri nets can have an exact mathematical definition of their execution semantics.

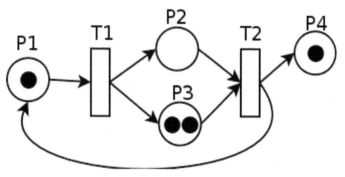

Figure 4 Petri nets.

o   Markov chain: uses transitions that can go from one state to another for a finite number of possible states. The next state depends only on the current state and not on the entire past, this is named memoryless. The transitions are the changes of states, and there are probabilities associated with various state-changes called transition probabilities. The next state depends only on the current state of the system, and not on the previous steps.

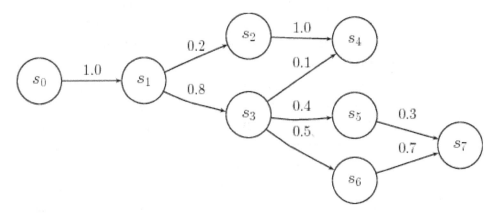

Figure 5 Example of a Markov chain

3.4   Reliability

Reliability is defined as the continuity of service, or the probability that a system or service remains operable for a specific period of time, or the ability of a system to perform its required functions under stated conditions for a specific period of time (Sterbenz, et al. 2010). And it is normally measured in terms of the MTTF, or mean time to failure, based on data that is accumulated after a long use of the systems based on experience on that system. The formula used for measure the reliability is defined (Dhillon 2003) by:

$$R(t) = 1 - \int_0^t f(t)dt$$

Equation 1 Reliability measure

Where R(t) is the reliability at time t and f(t) is the failure density function. This is used together with the reliabilities networks (Dhillon 2003), including the series, parallel, series-parallel, parallel-series and standby systems. These concepts, which are used for all kind of systems for calculating reliability, can be used in the model described later.

In figure 5 (Weibull 2010) shows the "time to failure" as the time period of correct operation as continuous random variable X. The cumulative distribution function cdf(t) for t will show the probability of failure before t, or the unreliability that is in red. And 1-cdf(t) will show the probability of a failure after t, that is the Reliability function, or time to failure. Usually Poisson distributions are used to represent it, but there are issues these distributions are memory less, that not always represent the failures. To solve this, Weibull distributions can be used.

Reliability and availability values for each fault tolerance mechanism related to server faults are calculated using a Markov model.

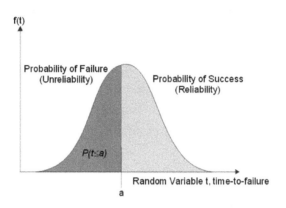

In order to have the reliability function we need to have the failure rate λ of the component/system as described in the equation 2. Once we have the failure rate, we can basically have the reliability of that component/system.

$$R(t) = P(X > t) = 1 - F(t) = e^{-\lambda x}$$

$$F(x) = 1 - e^{-\lambda x}$$

Equation 2 Reliability function for exponential failure distribution

3.5   Failures

A failure is any inability of a system to carry out its specified function. This can be any part, subsystem, system or equipment that can be individually considered and separately tested. According to Dummer, Winton and Toodley [Dummer 1997] the failures of an item can be classified in these ways:

- Causes of failure:
  - *Misuse failure:* Failures attributable to the application of stresses beyond the stated capabilities of the item.

- o *Inherent weakness failure* or *latent defect:* Failures attributable to weakness inherent in the item itself when subjected to stresses within the stated capabilities of that item.
- Duration of the Failure:
  - o Permanent failure: no possibility for repairing or replacement
  - o Recoverable Failure: back in operation after a fault is recovered
  - o Transient Failure: no mayor recovery action, short duration
- Effect of the failure:
  - o Functional failure: system does not operate according to its specification
  - o Performance failure: performance or SLA specifications not met
- Times of failure:
  - o *Sudden failure:* Failures that could not be anticipated by prior examination.
  - o *Gradual failure:* Failures that could be anticipated by prior examination.
- Degrees of failure:
  - o *Partial failure:* Failures resulting from deviations in characteristics beyond specified limits not such as to cause complete lack of the required function.
  - o *Complete failure:* Failures resulting from deviations in characteristic(s) beyond specified limits such as to cause complete lack of the required function. The limits referred to in this category are special limits for this purpose.
- Combinations of failures:
  - o *Catastrophic:* Failures that are both sudden and complete.
  - o *Degradation:* Failures that are both gradual and partial.

These classifications are focus on mechanical systems, but the reliability concepts can be used in computer systems, and in the same way in cloud services. As an example in the case of a SCADA system that can be managed using cloud services for non-vital parts of a system in an electric plant, let's imagine that a bug in the system makes that service fail when some values are sent to the service. At that point that service stops responding, the failure can be considered a latent defect, and a gradual because the failure could be anticipated due to prior examination. For this case less imagine that the failure is affecting only the system that is used for measure values of the one of the processes of the system, being a partial failure according to the classification. Finally, according to this classification, the failure can be considered a Degradation combination of failures. There are more classifications, and some will be presented here.

Figure 6 (Pan 1999)shows the typical curves for the failure rates of hardware and software. The failure rate in hardware goes up again due to the wear out of the hardware. The software depends mainly on the bug fixing due to the new integration of software or upgrades of software.

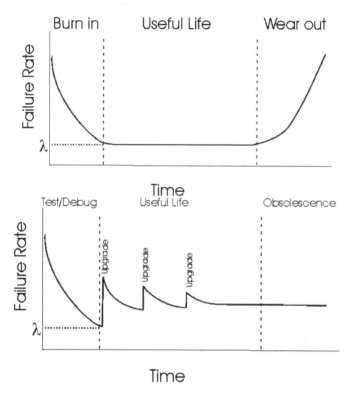

Figure 7 Bathtub curves for Hardware and software reliability (Pan 1999)

When building systems that are tolerant to faults, it is important to define the fault model that will be used, where is defined what type of faults the system will tolerate, defining the source and type of faults. Can be based on the nature of the faults (accidental/intentional), if is associated to phenomenological causes (physical or natural/ human), boundaries of the system (internal/external), phase of creation (design/operational), and the temporal persistence (permanent/temporary).

In cloud or distributed systems two of the most common types of faults are the crash and the byzantine faults. The crash faults produce the system components to completely stop working or remain inactive during the failure (power outage, hard disk crash). In the byzantine faults the system components behave randomly or maliciously during failure, causing the system to behave unpredictably.

Usually testing is used to probe the reliability of a system, but it is important to remember that testing can only prove the presence of faults, not their absence.

The most broadly adopted techniques to achieve fault tolerance against crash faults and byzantine faults are as follows in cloud computing are:

Checkpoint and restart: Based on some parameters such as time or number of instructions, the system state is saved. When the system experiences a failure, it is restored to the last saved correct state using the latest checkpoint information. This normally is more efficient that restarting the system from start.

Monitoring and checking: Runtime monitoring is used to check, verify, and ensure that the system is working properly.

Redundancy (in some cases called also replication of components): This is one of the most used in cloud computing systems. Critical system components are duplicated using additional hardware, software or network resources so a copy of the critical components is available even after a failure occurs. Redundancy mainly can be active or passive, but there are different variances such semi-active. In active all resources are working at the same time, while in passive replication only one resource is active and the others take over when the primary resource fails. In semi-active all nodes are active but only the output of the primary node is used, the replicas are ready to be used in case there is a failure. As an example, a system with passive redundancy can tolerate only crash faults, whereas a system using active replication with $3f+1$ replicas is capable of tolerating byzantine faults. The improvement of the fault tolerance of a system will imply to increase the usage of resources. We will need to take into account the type of fault tolerance model, the resource consumption and the performance needed in the system.

In standard on-premises models, redundancy has been done duplicating sets of hardware, software, and networking, for example as a cluster in a single data center or distributed across multiple data centers. But when using cloud services, we need to take into account not only the software running in the cloud provider environment, but also the redundancy between the cloud and us and the redundancy of the provider itself. There are different approaches or strategies and will depend of the cloud service model used (e.g. PaaS will provide most of the times this redundancy itself).

The most common redundancy approaches used are:

- Active/active — Traffic intended for a failed node is either passed onto an existing node or load balanced across the remaining nodes. Used when the nodes utilize a homogeneous software configuration.

- Active/passive — fully redundant instance of each node, which is only brought online when its associated primary node fails. This configuration typically requires the most extra hardware.

- N+1 — Provides a single extra node that is brought online to take over the role of the node that has failed. In the case of heterogeneous software configuration on each primary node, the extra node must be universally capable of assuming any of the roles of the primary nodes it is responsible for. This normally refers to clusters which have multiple services running simultaneously; in the single service case, this degenerates to active/passive.

- N+M — In cases where a single cluster is managing many services, having only one dedicated failover node may not offer sufficient redundancy. In such cases, more than one (M) standby servers are included and available. The number of standby servers is a tradeoff between cost and reliability requirements.

- N-to-1 — allows the failover standby node to become the active one temporarily, until the original node can be restored or brought back online, at which point the services or instances must be failed-back to it in order to restore high availability.

- N-to-N — A combination of active/active and N+M, N to N redistributes the services, instances or connections from the failed node among the remaining active nodes, thus eliminating (as with active/active) the need for a 'standby' node, but introducing a need for extra capacity on all active nodes.

3.6   Critical Systems

The term system will refer here to the entity that will be studied with a specific function, behaviour and a particular structure formed by a number of components or subsystems, which interact under the control of a design. The term critical systems in this work are used to define two types of systems:

- "Mission critical systems": the business will be affected seriously if the system fails.

- "Safety critical systems": someone can get harmed if the system fails, like in an airplane or some medical devices

It is important for these systems to have high levels of resilience and reliability, mainly for the safety ones where downtime could imply losses of lives, but as well for the mission critical systems, where the cost to the organization is huge as can been seen in table 1.

Sector/organization	Average Cost per hour of downtime
Brokerage operations in finance	$6.5 million
Credit car authorization	$2.6 million
Home catalog sales	$90.000
Airline reservation	$89.500

Table 1 Average costs per hour of downtime. (Gartner 1998)

There is now a trend to implement these types of systems with commercial off the shelf components mainly driven by trying to cut the costs and get advantage in performance. As well there is a tendency to implement these solutions with software instead of hardware redundancy approach, as it was done in the past. It is not affordable to use specialized components anymore, so more standard components and software is being used, and at the same time there is the need to improve the dependability in these systems.

Other two important concepts in resilience are fault domains and upgrade domains. A fault domain is a set of machines that can fail simultaneously, and are usually defined by physical properties such a rack with servers. Fault domains limit the location of services based on known hardware/software boundaries and the likelihood that a particular type of outage will affect a set of machines. Upgrade domains instead define a physical set of services that are updated by the system at the same time.

3.7   Cloud Computing

Before starting to define reliability for a cloud computing system, some concepts regarding to cloud computing will be explained. The term Cloud Computing is normally used for both applications, platforms and infrastructure delivered as services over the Internet and the hardware and systems software in the datacentres that provide those services. Some people believe that cloud computing is a variation of utility computing and that the term is a new way of naming services that have been in the market for a long time like hosting.

There are differences with the previous way of creating Information services; especially in the way we manage the infrastructure. In cloud computing we have the possibility of using different infrastructure building blocks, than can go from virtual servers to applications, usually in the form of open source technologies such as Mysql or Mongodb, that could help us to create the infrastructure needed in small time intervals.

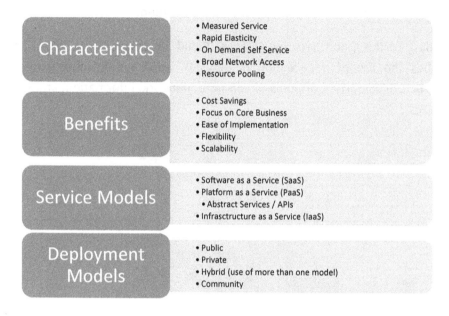

Figure 8 NIST Cloud Definition

The main characteristics of cloud computing services as can be seen in Figure 18 are:

- Self-service Provisioning by the customers, usually request of new services is done very quick, and in a similar way for decommissioning of services.
- Device and location independency, so the services can be accessed from everywhere and using almost any device.
- Standardized interfaces or standardized APIs to provide link of the cloud services with their own services, but this is not always true, as not too many vendors currently provide this type of standards.
- Elasticity and scalability, so the resource allocation gets bigger or smaller depending on the required demand. Usually different tenants use the services. It can be differentiated between horizontal and vertical scalability. Horizontal scalability refers to the amount of instances to satisfy, whereas vertical scalability refers to the size of the instances

themselves and thus implicit to the amount of resources required sustaining the size.

- Pay as you use billing model, so the customer is charged based on the utilization of resources during a specific period. This offers to the customer a low barrier entry point and no need for big capital expenditure in ICT infrastructure. This is done by moving from the usual capital upfront investment model to an operational expense.

According to the Cloud Security Alliance (Cloud Security Alliance 2011) "cloud describes the use of a collection of services, applications, information, and infrastructure comprised of pools of compute, network, information, and storage resources".

Figure 9 Layers of the different Services offered

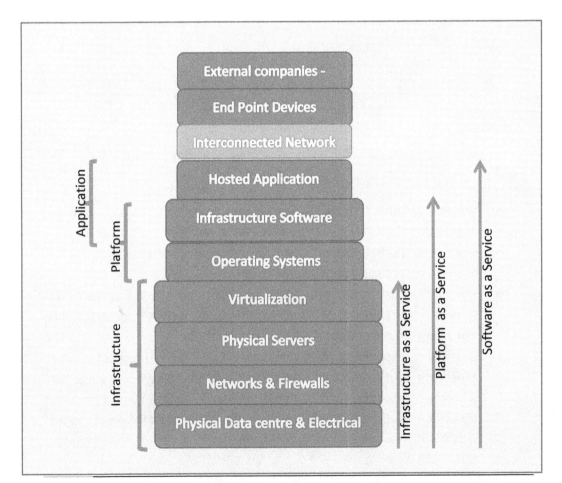

Other characteristics of cloud computing are:

- Availability: It is achieved mainly introducing redundancy for services and data so failures can be masked transparently. Fault tolerance also involves the ability to introduce new redundancy in an online, non-intrusively manner.With increasing concurrent access, availability is particularly achieved through replication of data / services, and distributing them across different resources to achieve load-balancing. This can be regarded as the original essence of scalability in cloud systems.
- Reliability should be built into a cloud system. Reliability represents the capability to ensure constant operation of the system without disruption, i.e. no loss of data. Reliability is typically achieved through redundant resource utilisation, in most cases moving reliability aspects from hardware to a software-based solution.
- Agility and adaptability: Including on-time reaction to changes such as environmental conditions, amount of requests and size of resources. It can be compared to what power providers and power distribution companies do to adapt to the changing demand, day vs night ([USTUTT-HLRS] and Editors: Keith Jeff ery [ERCIM] 2009).

Organizations that use cloud computing systems usually tend to use fewer resources (on-demand, pay-as-you-go) and use cheaper resources (off-hours at lower rates).

As we have seen cloud computing is based on a layer approach. This means that failures in a specific layer normally would affect layers above that layer, implying that failures in the infrastructure layer (IaaS) will have higher impact. In order to find out the failure behavior and impact of component failures in these layers usually analytical models such as Markov chains or fault tree analysis are used.

3.8   Cloud Service Models

There are different service offerings of cloud services, figure 19 shows what components used each of these models and the main ones are:

3.8.1   Communication as a Service (CaaS)

Usually an outsource solution of the enterprise communications where the providers manage the software and the hardware for delivering diverse communication and collaboration services, and the integration with other services like email. The services offered are instant messaging (IM), voice over IP (VOIP), video conferencing, communication services anywhere and collaboration tools like virtual meetings. In some cases this model is considered as a kind of Software as a Service (SaaS), essentially because some people see the video conferencing or virtual meetings like a specific type of software that is provided as a Service to users. But there are some differences with the SaaS, like the integration at infrastructure level with some voice telephony services and PBX in organizations. These models present advantages especially to small and medium size organizations because of the main characteristics of cloud services, that here involves no capital expenditures, reduce the risk of obsolescence because the services are updated by the vendor, service and support levels are very high, and usually a guaranteed business continuity.

3.8.2   Software as a Service (SaaS)

This would be the higher layer of the services offered, and usually is an application that is offered as a service, sharing the same main characteristics that the rest cloud computing services like multitenancy, elasticity and self-provisioning. There are many examples of these services, and almost all the most popular software is available now as SaaS (MS Office, mail, salesforce,…). In this case the customer uses the applications running on a cloud infrastructure of the provider, and the customer does not manage this underlying infrastructure (networks, servers, storage, Oss or the application itself)

3.8.3   Platform as a Service (PaaS)

In this case, what is offered is usually a complete development platform where the developers can develop their own systems using all the characteristics of cloud services. In this case most of the characteristics of the cloud are used as the systems are done precisely for running in a cloud platform. Most popular ones are Microsoft Azure that extends their development suite and SQL Server products to be deployed on their datacentre systems and Google App Engine, that has two main programming languages available, Python and Java.

These services provide a wide range of services and APIs for developers like authentication and Single sing on, Database and file-similar storage. There different vendors like Google app engine, Amazon Web Services Microsoft's Azure Services Platform, Salesforce.com's Force.com Platform, Sina.com's Sina App Engine (Chinese) and Heroku.

3.8.4   Infrastructure as a Service (IaaS)

Here the customer has the possibility of provision networks, processing, storage and servers that can run specific operating systems. Charging is done based on processing units, memory and storage allocated, as well as network utilization. Currently this is the most popular cloud service for organizations, due to the compatibility with current systems, as is basically a new virtual server with an OS installed. Virtualization made easy providing these services, this combined with the widespread Internet access made possible that infrastructure could be used and manage on remote datacentres. With IaaS organizations can build new versions of applications or environments remotely, some providers give the opportunity of not only creating virtual servers, but complete environments with networking components like virtual switches, firewalls, specific vlans and multiple virtual servers.

3.9   Cloud Deployment Models

Depending on the kind of cloud deployment, the cloud may have limited private computing resources, or may have access to large quantities of remotely public accessed resources. The following deployment models present a number of trade-offs in how customers can control their resources, and the scale, cost, and availability of resources.

• Private cloud. The cloud infrastructure is operated exclusively for an organization. It may be managed by the organization or a third party and may exist on premise or off premise.

• Community cloud. The cloud infrastructure is shared by several organizations and supports a specific community that has shared requirements (e.g., mission, security requirements, policy and compliance considerations). It may be managed by the organizations or a third party and may exist on premise or off premise.

• Public cloud. The cloud infrastructure is made available to the general public or a large industry group and is owned by an organization selling cloud services.

• Hybrid cloud. The cloud infrastructure is a composition of two or more clouds (private, community, or public) that remain unique entities but that are bound together by standardized or proprietary technology enabling data and application portability.

• On-site private cloud. The security perimeter for this deployment model extends around both the subscriber's on-site resources and the private cloud's resources. The private cloud may be centralized at a single subscriber site or may be distributed over several subscriber sites. The subscriber implements the security perimeter, which will not guarantee control over the private cloud's resources, but will enable the subscriber to exercise control over resources entrusted to the on-site private cloud.

3.10   Standards for Cloud Computing

As with all new technologies, one of the main issues is to have good standards that permit the interoperability. Currently there are a few initiatives by different organizations in order to have standards for all the current issues but mainly for the interoperability, and others that could affect directly to reliability. I have included information related the main efforts by the main organizations. I have used extensively information from all these proposals for this work. There is as well the proposal of the opencloud manifesto [opencloud manifesto], it is not a standard, but a definition of how a future open cloud should be.

3.10.1   IEEE P2302

The Institute for Electrical and Electronics Engineers (IEEE) has two draft standards for cloud computing portability and interoperability, the standards are IEEE P2301, Draft Guide for Cloud Portability and Interoperability Profiles, and IEEE P2302, Draft Standard for Inter-cloud Interoperability and Federation.

The first standard, IEEE P2301 provides profiles of existing and in-progress cloud computing standards in critical areas such as application, portability, management, and interoperability interfaces, as well as file formats and operation conventions. It permits to help users in procuring, developing, building, and using standards-based cloud computing products and services, enabling better portability, increased commonality, and greater interoperability across the industry.

The second one, IEEE P2302 defines essential topology, protocols, functionality, and governance required for reliable cloud-to-cloud interoperability and federation. The standard helps build an economy of scale among cloud product and service providers that remains transparent to users and applications.

3.10.2 Open Grid Forum (OGF) – Open Cloud Computing Interface (OCCI) working group

The open Grid forum is an organization that sets standards about grid, cloud and advance distributed computing. According to OGF, OGF partners and participants throughout the international arena use these standards to champion architectural blueprints related to cloud and grid computing and the associated software development. Different organizations use the resulting clouds and grids as production distributed architectures built on these features to collaborate in areas as diverse as scientific data processing, drug discovery, cancer research, financial risk analysis, visualization and product design.

The Open Cloud Computing Interface (OCCI) is a general-purpose set of specifications for cloud-based interactions with resources in a way that is explicitly vendor-independent, platform-neutral and can be extended to solve a broad variety of problems in cloud computing. OCCI provides a protocol and API design components for all kinds of cloud management tasks. The work was originally initiated to create a remote management API for IaaS model based services, allowing for the development of interoperable tools for common tasks including deployment, autonomic scaling and monitoring. The current release of the Open Cloud Computing Interface is suitable to serve many other models in addition to IaaS, including e.g. PaaS and SaaS.

3.10.3 National Institute of Standards and Technology (NIST)

The National Institute of Standards and Technology (NIST), is a non-regulatory agency of the United States department of commerce that promotes US innovations and industrial competitiveness. NIST has prepared a working definition of cloud computing, and is preparing more information on the subject. The current document gives information about cloud architectures, security, and deployment for federal governments.

NIST is working as well in the Standards Acceleration to Jumpstart Adoption of Cloud Computing (SAJACC), in order to drive the formation of high-quality cloud computing standards by providing worked examples showing how key use cases can be supported on cloud systems that implement a set of documented and public cloud system specifications.

The SAJACC initiative is developing and maintaining a set of cloud system use cases through an open and on-going process engaging industry, other Government agencies, and academia. Simultaneously, the SAJACC initiative will collect and generate cloud system specifications through a similarly open and on-going process.

The SAJACC initiative will develop tests that show the extent to which specific use cases can be supported by cloud systems that implement documented and public cloud system specifications, and will publish test results on the SAJACC web portal (this web site).

3.10.4   Cloud Security Alliance – CSA

The Cloud Security Alliance was created to promote the use of best practices for providing security assurance within Cloud Computing, and provide education on the uses of Cloud Computing to help secure all other forms of computing.

Currently they have prepared a few initiatives in order to help customers to improve the use of cloud services, most of them are reports:

- The Security Guidance for Critical areas of focus in cloud computing (CSA 2009) covers the key issues and provides advice for both customers and providers within fifteen strategic domains, including information about cloud architecture, governing in the cloud and operating in the cloud. There is a domain dedicated to incident response, notification and remediation only, but there is not specific information about reliability for cloud environments.
- The Cloud Security Alliance Controls Matrix (CM) (CSA 2011) is specifically designed to provide fundamental security principles to guide cloud vendors and to assist prospective cloud customers in assessing the overall security risk of a cloud provider.
- Top Threats to Cloud Computing (CSA 2010): provide needed context to assist organizations in making educated risk management decisions regarding their cloud adoption strategies.
- CloudAudit provides a common interface and namespace that allows cloud computing providers to automate the Audit, Assertion, Assessment, and Assurance (A6) of their infrastructure (IaaS), platform (PaaS), and application (SaaS) environments and allow authorized consumers of their services to do likewise via an open, extensible and secure interface and methodology.

3.10.5 Distributed Management Task Force – DMTF

The DMTF is an industry organization that develops, maintains and promotes systems management standards in enterprise IT environments. These standards allow for building systems management infrastructure components in a platform-independent and technology-neutral way. By creating the open industry standards, DMTF helps enable systems management interoperability between IT products from different manufacturers or companies.

They have develop different standards related to cloud computing:

- Open Virtualization Format (OVF), an standard for packaging and deploying virtual appliances in an open, secure, portable, efficient and extensible way. The main one is DSP0243 Open Virtualization Format (OVF) V1.1.0. OVF has been designated as ANSI INCITS 469 2010

- The DMTF Open Cloud Standards Incubator is focused on standardizing interactions between cloud environments by developing cloud management use cases, architectures and interactions. This work was completed in July 2010. The work has now transitioned to the Cloud Management Working Group.

- Interoperable Clouds White Paper: DSP-IS0101 Cloud Interoperability White Paper V1.0.0. This white paper describes a snapshot of the work being done in the DMTF Open Cloud Standards Incubator, including use cases and reference architecture as they relate to the interfaces between a cloud service provider and a cloud service consumer.

- Architecture for Managing Clouds White Paper, DSP-IS0102 Architecture for Managing Clouds White Paper V1.0.0. This white paper is one of two Phase 2 deliverables from the DMTF Cloud Incubator and describes the reference architecture as it relates to the interfaces between a cloud service provider and a cloud service consumer. The goal of the Incubator is to define a set of architectural semantics that unify the interoperable management of enterprise and cloud computing.

- Use Cases and Interactions for Managing Clouds White Paper, DSP-IS0103 Use Cases and Interactions for Managing Clouds White Paper V1.0.0. This document is one of two documents that together describe how standardized interfaces and data formats can be used to manage clouds. This document focuses on use cases, interactions, and data formats.

- Cloud Management Working Group (CMWG) The CMWG will develop a set of prescriptive specifications that deliver architectural semantics as well as implementation details to achieve interoperable management of clouds between service requestors/developers and providers. This WG will propose a resource model that at minimum captures the key artefacts identified in the Use Cases and Interactions for Managing Clouds document produced by the Open Cloud Incubator.

3.10.6 European Telecommunications Standards Institute (ETSI)

The European Telecommunications Standards Institute (ETSI) is a not-for-profit organization that produces globally-applicable standards for Information and Communications Technologies (ICT), including fixed, mobile, radio, converged, broadcast and internet technologies. It is recognized by the European Union as a European Standards Organization. Related to cloud computing, they have created the ETSI TC Cloud.

The goal of ETSI TC CLOUD (previously TC GRID) is to address issues associated with the convergence between IT (Information Technology) and Telecommunications. The focus is on scenarios where connectivity goes beyond the local network. This includes not only Grid computing but also the emerging commercial trend towards Cloud computing which places particular emphasis on ubiquitous network access to scalable computing and storage resources.

Since TC CLOUD has particular interest in interoperable solutions in situations which involve contributions from both the IT and Telecom industries, the emphasis is on the Infrastructure as a Service (IaaS) delivery model. TC GRID focuses on interoperable applications and services based on global standards and the validation tools to support these standards. Evolution towards a coherent and consistent general purpose infrastructure is envisaged. This will support networked IT applications in business, public sector, academic and consumer environments.

3.10.7 Open Cloud Consortium (OCC)

The Open Cloud Consortium (OCC) is a member driven organization that develops reference implementations, benchmarks and standards for cloud computing. The

OCC operates clouds testbeds, such as the Open Cloud Testbed and the OCC Virtual Network Testbed. The OCC also manages cloud computing infrastructure to support scientific research, such as the Open Science Data Cloud.

The Open Cloud Consortium (OCC)

- Supports the development of standards for cloud computing and frameworks for interoperating between clouds;

- develops benchmarks for cloud computing; and

- supports reference implementations for cloud computing, preferably open source reference implementations.

The OCC has a particular focus in large data clouds. It has developed the MalStone Benchmark for large data clouds and is working on a reference model for large data clouds.

3.11   Cloud Toolkits

3.11.1   VMWare vCloud

Currently utilizes VSphere 4 / VCloud for private cloud installation. With a huge virtualization market, it offers an easy path to hybrid cloud due to the fact that uses the same technology that most of current organizations are using for virtualising the datacenters, and is based in vSphere. It is based on the ESX hypervisor that manages a host, and many ESX are managed to create a clusters and a private cloud. The hybrid model only applies if the cloud vendor uses VMWARE vcloud solution. VMWare offers features such as high availability, fault-tolerance, or distributed resource scheduling.

3.11.2   Eucalyptus

It is a private cloud infrastructure based on XEN / KVM. It offers Amazon EC2 and S3 interfaces. Eucalyptus uses KVM as its underlying virtualization technology. Amazon as an example uses XEN. Eucalyptus stands for Elastic Utility Computing Architecture for Linking Your Programs To Useful Systems. It is mainly composed of 5 components (Daniel Nurmi 2009):

Cloud Controller (CLC) is a web interface used by administrators to obtain credentials, create user accounts, manage the machine images, and configure the services. There is one CLC per Eucalyptus installation, and it makes high-level scheduling decisions asking the controllers of the cluster to implement them as well as checking available resources.

Walrus Storage Controller (WS3) provides the storage for the images and other files; this is compatible with Amazon S3 storage.

Elastic Block Storage (EBS) Controller is used for the persistent block devices (similar to disk partitions) that will be mounted into virtual servers.

Cluster Controller (CC) interacts between the CLC and the node controller, receiving the request from the CLC to allocate machines images, and decides where in the cluster will be deployed.

Node Controller manages the execution, inspection and termination of the machine instances on one node (the physical server) within a cluster (one node controller per physical back-end machine in the cluster).

3.11.3 Nimbus
Private cloud based on SGE / PBS cluster. It provides Amazon EC2 interfaces.It provides a private IaaS cloud compatible with Amazon (AWS) interfaces. Can be configured to use external schedulers.

3.11.4 OpenNebula
It is project started by researchers of the University of Chicago and Madrid in 2008. It is an open source solution for private and hybrid clouds, focusing on integrating different clouds in a single system, supporting different hypervisors and public cloud providers.

3.11.5 Red Hat Enterprise Virtualization (RHEV)
The hypervisor is based on the Kernel-Based Virtual Machine (KVM) based on a subset of Red Hat Enterprise Linux (RHEL). It supports live migration, image management and virtual networking.

3.11.6 Microsoft Hyper-V
The Microsoft offer supports live migration and cluster-aware file system, but it is still behind the other big players in functionality, partly due to be new compare with his competitors. It is provided as part of Windows 2008 R2 or as standalone hypervisor.

3.11.7 Citrix XenServer

It is based on the Xen hypervisor and supports live migration with Xenmotion, and a multi-server management systems.

3.11.8 Comparative of Cloud Toolkits

The following table shows at the time this work is prepared the status of the different cloud toolkits. This is as a reference only and can change due to the speed the different providers are changing their products to cope with the demands of the market.

Characteristics	VMware vSphere	Eucalyptus	RHEV	Nimbus	OpenNebula	XenServer	Hyper-V
Hypervisor	VMware	Xen, KVM, VMware	KVM	Xen	Xen, KVM, VMware	Xen, Hyper-V	Hyper-V, Xen
API	vCloud API	Implements different APIs	Different: Deltacloud, REST	RM API	OpenNebula API	Xen Server API	Hyper-V API
License	Proprietary	BSD Proprietary	Proprietary	Apache 2	Apache 2	Propietary, some free editions	Proprietary
High Availability	Yes	No	Yes	No	No	Yes	Yes
Supported Guest OSs	Windows, Linux	Depending on Hypervisor	RedHat, Windows	Depending on Hypervisor	Depending on Hypervisor	Windows, RedHat, SUSE, Debian	Windows, RedHat, SUSE
Hybrid Cloud	Yes	Limited	No	Partially	Partially	No	No
Live Migration	Yes	Yes	Yes	Yes	Yes	Yes	Yes
Scheduling	Yes	Limited	Yes	External	External	Not applicable	Not applicable

Table 2 Comparative cloud toolkits

3.12 Main Cloud vendors

These are some of the current bigger vendors of cloud services in the market. It will be impossible to have an exhaustive list, as new vendors are being added to the list every day. I choose these vendors not based on the volume but on the different strategies for offering cloud services, as I think these will be illustrative.

3.12.1 IBM's Blue Cloud

IBM Smart Business Development and Test on the IBM Cloud is designed to augment and enhance software development and delivery capabilities, particularly in large enterprises. The cloud was launch initially with more than a petabyte of data.

3.12.2   Amazon AWS

Amazon is mainly specialized in IaaS. It offers it through Amazon Web Services (AWS): Amazon Elastic Compute Cloud (EC2), Amazon SimpleDB, Amazon CloudFront, Amazon SQS, and. AWS offers compute as EC2 (Elastic Compute Cloud) and storage as S3 (Simple Storage Service). RDS (Relational Database Service) is "database as a service," hiding many of the complications of databases behind a service layer. CloudFront is the Content Distribution Network (CDN) offered by AWS. It helps to distribute static, dynamic, and streaming content to different places in the world. Simple Email Service (SES) is used to send mails (normally for very large batches).

3.12.3   Google Cloud Platform

Google offers both IaaS, PaaS & SaaS services. As SaaS it offers Google Apps: a web-based communication, collaboration & security apps which includes, Gmail, Google Calendar, Google Talk, Google Docs & Google Sites. Google provides as well GovCloud, which will host Google Apps in a separate data environment with enhanced encryption for meeting state and government security standards.

As PaaS it offers Google App Engine: a platform for developing and hosting web applications in Google-managed data centers. Currently, the supported programming languages are Python and Java (by extension other JVM languages are also supported). The application is built using Google's PaaS and Google handles deploying code to a cluster, monitoring, failover, and launching application instances as necessary.

The newest offer is Google compute engine. Compute Engine is an infrastructure as a service that lets you run your large-scale computing workloads on Linux virtual machines hosted on Google's infrastructure.

3.12.4   Microsoft Azure

The Microsoft cloud Azure is focused in PaaS. It offers Azure, a Windows-as-a-service platform consisting of the operating system and developer services that can be used to build Web-hosted applications. Visual Studio has all the features needed to code, debug, and deploy the cloud service.

3.12.5   Vmware Vcloud Datacenter Services

VMware vCloud Datacenter Services is based in IaaS services offered by VMware-certified service providers. The idea here is that other cloud vendors (like Colt) provide cloud services to organisations based on VMware hypervisor technology, in this way, the customers can migrate virtual services from their datacentres to the one in the vendor and change between vendors easily.

	Microsoft Azure	Google App Engine	VMware	Amazon Web Services
Architecture	.NET code provided by the customer for the front end and back end. Code is deployed in Windows 2008 virtual machines.	Customer writes web applications in python or Java according to Google app engine restrictions and the application is deployed in Google infrastructure.	Deploy and move virtual machines into datacentres that support their vcloud model.	Customer deploys the xen virtual machine image into the Amazon Elastic Compute Cloud (EC2). There are APIs to manage these virtual machines.
Load Balancing	Yes	Yes	Yes	Not
Storage	Application Storage and SQL Services	Database Storage APIs	Default virtual machine storage	Simple Storage Service (S3) and SimpleDB
VM	-Microsoft Common Language Runtime (CLR) VM; common intermediate form executed in managed environment - Machines are provisioned based on declarative descriptions (e.g. which "roles" can be replicated); automatic load balancing	Predefined application structure and framework; programmer-provided "handlers" written in Python, all persistent state stored in MegaStore (outside Python code) _ Automatic scaling up and down of computation and storage; network and server failover; all consistent with 3-tier Web app structure	VMware virtual machine format.	-x86 using Xen VM -Computation elasticity allows scalability, but developer must build the machinery, or third party VAR such as RightScale must provide it
Tied to vendor's datacenter	Yes	Yes	VMs can be hosted on any partner that supports vcloud.	Yes

Table 3 Different Cloud vendors

3.13   GovCloud and Use of Cloud Computing by public sector

Public organizations have been slow in the utilization of cloud services compared to private ones, especially in Europe. Some reasons for their reluctance to use cloud services are similar to the ones of private companies. For example, security and data protection, but others are more specific to public organizations, such as aversion to risk and the fact that current offerings are more focused on the requirements of private organizations. In the next sections some of these problems are presented and some possible solutions. There is not a silver bullet for cloud services in public organizations, but some models adapt better to public organizations' requirements than others. We will suggest what could be done for public organizations to attain the main goals of cloud computing (scalability, elasticity, self-provisioning, and pay-as-you-go charging).

3.13.1   Introduction

Governments are facing reduction in ICT budgets and at the same time demands for electronic services by users are increasing. One solution that is announced aggressively by all vendors is cloud computing. Cloud computing is not a new technology, but as described by Jackson (Kevin L. Jackson 2011) a new way of offering services taking into consideration business and economic models for providing and consuming ICT Services.

   This section tries to explain how the main characteristics of clouds could impact and benefit public organizations. In the second section, the different cloud models are explained with the pros and cons for public organizations. In a similar way section three explains the deployment models. Some challenges and benefits for public organizations are described in sections four and five. Section five is dedicated to the three main concerns about using cloud computing (security, confidentiality and availability) in public organizations, together with the integration of internal systems and especially identity management. In the following section (six), legal concerns are explained, including legal regulations and the "safe harbor" agreement (Commerce, US Deparment of 2010). In the last two sections (7 & 8) some concepts related to the use of cloud computing and how these could affect the way applications are used and deployed in public organizations are explained. Some conclusions and recommendations are presented to finish the chapter.

3.13.2 Cloud models

There are three different types of cloud models, with different use of the main cloud stack; as per Figure 10 Different types of cloud models and their respective cloud Stacks.

The Software as a Service (SaaS) concept is probably the easiest to use for most organizations, including the public sector. To use this service, only the accounts need to be created on the system, or connected to an internal organization identity management system. Once this is done, some basic configuration can be applied and the standard functionality of the service is ready to use. Good examples are SalesForce.com and Google Apps for Government (mail, calendar, sites, video), which have been certified for use by the American Government as defined by FISMA (Federal Information Security Management Act) (computer security division, FISMA Detailed Overview 2011) as described later. The main issue, apart from the standard ones, like security and data protection, is vendor lock-in. The problem is how to move the information to other vendors or return the information in house, as the system is highly customized by the vendor. All the main software companies are offering services like SAP and Microsoft 365. The benefits for the public sector are that standard software (office automation, mail, SAP, email) and citizen engagement services like wikis, blogs, social networking or website hosting (Chen 2010) can be used with minimum capital expenditure, removing the overhead costs of installing and maintaining these systems.

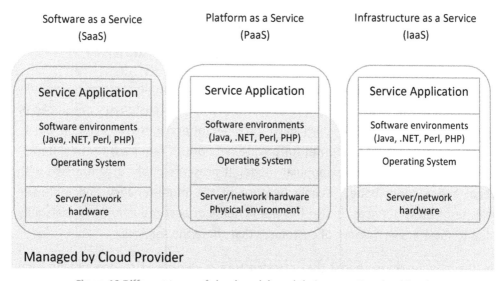

Figure 10 Different types of cloud models and their respective cloud Stacks

In the Platform as a Service model (PaaS) the application is created and administered by the customer, but runs on a software platform (databases, programing languages and middleware) that is managed by the cloud provider. Microsoft Azure and Google App Engine are examples of this model. If the application has been created properly the customer does not need to worry about all the infrastructure and software in the background, removing the need for investment in and maintenance of these technologies. For the public sector this type of software development represents a good opportunity to provide the specific applications needed by the public organization in a simple way. These cannot be provided with standard off-the-shelf software. An example is the use of Microsoft Azure by the European Environment Agency (EAA) with the project Eyeonearth (http://www.eyeonearth.eu/). Another use could be as a development and testing environment.

For the last model, Infrastructure as a Service (IaaS), most parts of the system (OS, middleware and application) are installed and managed by the customer. The vendor manages the hardware and the virtualization layer, permitting more independence from the vendor's technology. This has the drawback of requiring more maintenance work by the customer. The main benefit of this model is that if a public organization is using virtualization it is easy to move stand-alone servers to the cloud, but this is not always the case, as sometimes is not easy due to the integration with other systems in the organization.

3.13.3 Deployment models

The main deployment models for cloud computing are public, private, community and hybrid. But there are variations of these, like virtual private model.

In the public model the infrastructure is offered to multiple customers, typically over the Internet and usually it does not matter if the customers are public or private organizations. The third party provider offers these services on offsite locations, connected by Internet (or private networks if required) to the different customers. This is the most popular model. It presents public organizations with legal and security issues, mainly because of the multi-tenancy and multi-site nature of these services. It also has the benefits of cost reduction and scalability due to the massive number of customers that share the services.

In the private cloud model the infrastructure is dedicated to one organization where the service can be operated internally or by a third-party provider; the equipment being on or off site. This option offers a higher level of control, but it involves higher investment in expertise and resource management. Many organizations are starting to move to this model because some of the technologies that they use are moving in the direction of offering scalability, elasticity, self-service and chargeback models; examples are VMware vcloud or Oracle. The main benefit for public organizations is greater control of the environment, including data protection and security. This is an excellent way to test cloud technologies before moving to a community or public cloud, but can be expensive if only for private use

The third model is the community cloud, where the infrastructure is shared by several organizations with similar needs. This model makes it a good candidate for the public sector because they usually need a certain level of privacy or policy compliance, but using a private cloud would be too expensive. The main challenge is reaching an agreement between all the organizations for the service requirements and utilization. Even if the requirements and goals are common, different ICT departments need to agree and establish trust before moving certain services that are currently offered internally to third parties, because of the lack of control that this implies. The idea here is to share resources between agencies with similar ICT requirements. If each agency "does its own thing" in terms of cloud computing, we have not differed significantly from the current situation of each agency acquiring an individual solution for its IT needs. (Kevin L. Jackson 2011)

Other possible models can be a combination of two or more cloud models. In the end, even if the strategy of an organization is clearly to use one type of model, the reality is that they are using the public model for some services.

3.13.4 Challenges

If all these models have been tested by other organizations, why are more Public organizations not using them as well? Probably, the main challenges are security and legal ones, especially in public organizations in the EU with the Data Protection Directive. These will be treated separately in the next sections.

Another of the main challenges is the integration with current systems. Most of these public organizations have been using Information and Communication Technologies for a long time now. These systems have evolved over the years; in some cases from silos based on specific requirements or new legislation and using specific technology (like big relational database systems with Java applications running on application servers) that was compatible with the existing systems. Cloud services are not created with connection to internal systems in mind. This implies incompatibility and repetition of systems for the public organization. A new system that is completely independent from existing ones is a good candidate for using a cloud service. However, most often integration with existing services is required, rather than having 3 different instances of a product that do not communicate. The solution for this problem is for the ICT department to take a long-term strategy when moving to these services and to look for long term ROI.

Another challenge is the added cost of these technologies. The main advantages of cloud services are fast scalability and elasticity. This is especially useful for seasonal services like paying taxes online or when there is suddenly increased demand on services, such as requests for information about a new pandemic flu vaccine. However, the current systems are based on technologies that the public organization has made hardware, software and knowledge investments in. To move these services into a cloud environment where the use of this elasticity could be useful will usually require big changes to the software. In some cases it may even have to be completely re-written.

There will be services that cannot be easily migrated to the cloud in the short and medium term and this limits the possible cost savings due to the need to retain much of the present infrastructure. Again, the solution is a long-term strategy, creating new services that can work in a cloud model. To begin with, this will be more costly, as the previous services and new cloud services will need to be maintained simultaneously. Any outsourcing strategy the public organization has should also be considered. When outsourcing, some public organizations classify their services according to the following definitions: "Proprietary and Mission Critical"; these are not outsourced at all, "Non-Proprietary and Mission Critical" that are developed by another company and "Non-Proprietary" that can be outsourced. (Mutavdzi 2010). Another possible classification is internal sourcing, public-private partnership, externalization or privatization.

If the public organization's ICT department does not have a clear chargeback financial model, the number of systems and servers could grow rapidly as there is not a clear need to decommission systems because of their maintenance cost.

3.13.5 Benefits
The benefits for public organizations are similar to the ones experienced by private ones. The most misunderstood is cost and this is most often what drives

projects to move to a cloud. What usually happens is that costs are mainly moved from capital expenditure to operational expenditure. Whether there is any benefit depends on the type of services provided by the public organization.

Reducing the ICT headcount or reassigning staff to other tasks could be a long-term benefit, but if it is not handled properly it can create problems with dependency on the cloud vendors. As in private organizations, this is driven by a desire to focus resources on the core business. What happens is that there are fewer specific technical management tasks, but there must be more staff with knowledge of the new cloud models and management of Service Level Agreements.

Other direct benefits are the scalability, elasticity, self-provisioning and pay-as-you-go charging model. There may also be indirect benefits arising from the use of services associated with cloud technologies. For example, social interaction business models where work is performed with the help of the public. For public organizations this makes it easier to implement new service models that give users more control and encourage greater participation. An example is eyeonearh.eu, featuring applications where the data are supplied directly by users who can interact easily with the systems, making them more transparent to citizens and less expensive for the public organization to maintain.

Access to public data and/or services is made easier, so external organizations or even individuals can create value added systems using the software and data available. For example, Matthew Somerville has built a website using Microsoft Azure cloud that shows live Underground train positions, using Transport for London's data.

3.13.6 Security

Security, along with legal regulations, is probably the most important issues for public organizations. The same principles apply as for other non-cloud systems, but the main difference is the lack of control of the cloud services and the secrecy of how these systems are managed by the cloud providers. In the cloud model, the data owner is still the public organization, but the custodian is the cloud provider. The provider has the responsibility of ensuring the data owner's security requirements are always met.

Normally the auditing and compliance requirements of public organizations will be more difficult to achieve in a cloud environment. Access to log files and other auditing information may be difficult. In the cloud, some of the traditional controls are managed through contracts and SLAs. The level of security will depend on the type of cloud model used; it will be more similar to the traditional systems in the case of IaaS, where there is more control, with less control in the SaaS model. A proper information security risk assessment has to be done, whatever the model, to identify and manage all substantial risks. Even if it is possible to transfer the liability using specific contracts, the accountability will still be with the public organization. A clear policy for dealing with security incidents should be in the contracts and SLAs with the vendors.

Physical security is not normally an issue, because cloud providers' data centres are usually better protected and prepared than those owned by public organizations. Vulnerability detection and patch management are normally difficult to manage than when using in-house systems. It is not easy to use vulnerability discovery tools to assess parts of the systems and this should only be done in cases where the cloud provider's Acceptable Use Policy permits. Other matters to consider include managing the backup and restoration of data and controlling the proper disposal of data and equipment. It may be possible to use encryption to increase the security of data. When using IaaS, encrypted storage can be used. The customer is responsible for most security controls, including the operating system, application patching, the backup and recovery of data, as well as hardening of the OS. With SaaS, the provider is responsible for most of the security controls and very little information on how this is done is usually shared. In the case of PaaS, the public organization is responsible for the security controls in their application.

The public organization is responsible for ensuring that the same testing criteria apply to the cloud system as for other internal applications, including the backup and recovery of the application code.

3.13.7 Confidentiality

When processing, storing and communicating sensitive information, the normal protection measures that the organization has for internal systems must be applied, plus the specific measures required for cloud services. Usually authentication, authorization, compartmentalization (limiting access to those on a need to know basis) and encryption are employed. Encryption normally can be applied in the PaaS (using specific APIs) and IaaS models (encrypted volumes).

It is important to know whether personal data that will be in the cloud is aggregated or whether it can identify individuals. This means knowing whether there will be data records that relate to one specific person (like name, address, etc). Special care should be taken regarding the retention and destruction of any data when no longer needed.

When using SaaS data is normally transmitted and received over the Internet and it is important to make sure this is done securely, for example by using SSL/TLS. When using the PaaS model communication methods should be checked to verify they are encrypted, but in this case it is the responsibility of the customer that creates the application, ideally using trusted cryptographic toolkits. In the IaaS model, the customer has more control over the use of cryptography. For example, by using encrypted volumes or specific vendor encryption. However, in most cases, encryption cannot prevent the cloud provider from accessing data that is processed in the cloud, though it can make such access more difficult..

3.13.8 Availability

When judged by the characteristics of reliability defined in Table 1, cloud services are often better than those managed internally by public organizations. When measuring or specifying availability it is necessary to take into account planned (like maintenance) and unplanned downtime. The availability offered by cloud providers varies, but is normally similar to three or four nines. This means 99.9% or 99.99% up time; a maximum of 8.77 hours or 53 minutes respectively of downtime per year.

Availability %	Downtime per year	Downtime per month	Downtime per week
90%	36.5 days	72 hours	16.8 hours
95%	18.25 days	36 hours	8.4 hours
97%	10.96 days	21.6 hours	5.04 hours
98%	7.30 days	14.4 hours	3.36 hours
99%	3.65 days	7.20 hours	1.68 hours
99.5%	1.83 days	3.60 hours	50.4 minutes
99.8%	17.52 hours	86.23 minutes	20.16 minutes

99.9% or "three nines"	8.76 hours	43.2 minutes	10.1 minutes
99.95%	4.38 hours	21.56 minutes	5.04 minutes
99.99% or "four nines"	52.56 minutes	4.32 minutes	1.01 minutes
99.999% or "five nines"	5.26 minutes	25.9 seconds	6.05 seconds
99.9999% or "six nines"	31.5 seconds	2.59 seconds	0.605 seconds
99.99999% or "seven nines"	3.15 seconds	.259 seconds	0.0605 seconds

Table 4 Availability percentage and downtime in seconds

Availability guarantees may be specified in the SLA, but it can be difficult to prove whether they are met. As an example, the SLA for Google's storage service states it will be available for 99.9% of the time in any billing month. If it is not, the customer receives a refund of up to 50% of the bill if availability fell below 95%.This could cause some customers to go out of business. How can the customer monitor the system in the cloud? Normally the provider controls this, however it is always necessary to monitor the system from the outside as well as collecting statistics from the customer environment.

There could be many reasons for low availability figures, such as modification of the service by the provider, denial of service attacks against the provider and even closure of the service. For this reason it is always important to consider interoperability from the outset; it may be necessary to move the service to another provider or bring it in-house. Vendor lock-in is lowest with IaaS, greater with PaaS and greatest with SaaS.

3.13.9 Identity Management and integration with internal systems

Another challenge when using cloud systems is how to manage user accounts and how to link the cloud systems with the ones running internally. For account management, the best solution is usually to link the accounts used by the cloud system to the internal user database at the public organization (for example, Active Directory). There are some systems that permit this, like Google Apps that can be tied to Active Directory or Blackberry ID management, but these are currently immature.

For IaaS, all user provisioning is done by the customer and normally integration of identity management and other types of integration are easy if there is a proper network connection between those systems. This normally implies a secure VPN connection between external and internal systems. In PaaS, the customer, being the developer, must implement the access control methods using the provider's tools and normally the user authentication and access control can be built in to the application using enterprise identity providers like IBM CA, OpenSSO, Oracle IAM or third-party identity service providers like Ping Identity and TriCipher. Another option for user authentication in PaaS is to use a provider supplied method, like Google Authenticator. In the case of SaaS, normally the customer must provision the users using the provider's tools. There are some third-party solutions that permit some integration between the provider's tools and internal ones, e.g. Ping Identity for Salesforce.

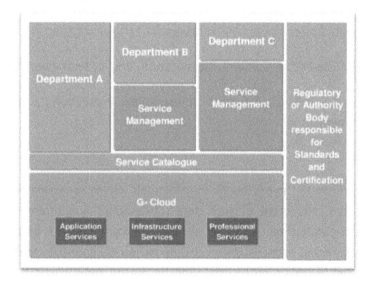

Figure 11 Service Catalogue in UK G-Cloud

Once the method for identity management has been decided upon, the interfaces between internal and external systems need to be addressed. Governments that are already using Service Oriented Architecture (SOA) will experience easy integration. It is important to carefully manage the interfaces between the implementations and any changes made to the services. This can be a huge challenge if it is not controlled properly through change and configuration management. (Mutavdzi 2010)

3.13.10 Legal Regulations

Legal requirements, especially those relating to data protection, are probably the most important consideration when public organizations plan to use cloud services. There are different legal regulations that can affect the use of external cloud services, the main ones are:

- EU: Data Protection Directive

- US: FISMA (Federal Information Security Management Act), HIPAA (Health Insurance Portability and Accountability Act of 1996)

- UK: Data Protection Act 1998; Computer Misuse Act 1990

- APEC (Asia-Pacific Economic Cooperation) Privacy Framework

- Canada: PIPEDA (Personal Information Protection and Electronic Documents Act)

The majority relate to the protection of individuals when processing personal data and to the free movement of such data (Christopher A. Cannin 2009). As an example, EU legislation had an effect around the world because of its provisions allowing "transfers of personal data . . . only to non-EU countries that provide an 'adequate' level of privacy protection". For this reason, before starting to plan any technical details of the system, it is important to have understood all possible legal implications and how these will be met in the cloud implementation. EU privacy regulations are stricter than many others and companies and public organizations in the EU may not send or store personal data outside the EU.

This is the geopolitics of cloud computing. An example of this is the opinion in early 2011 of the Danish Data Protection Authority on a notification from the Odense Municipality on the use of Google Apps for processing data related to educational activities because Odense would be unable to prove where the data was (Giannakaki 2011).

Another example is the US Patriot Act, where data that is in the US can be seized if required by the US government, even if the data is from another country and classified as confidential. Different governments around the world, such as the

Canadian, have forbidden the storage or processing of government data by US firms due to this act.

3.13.11 Safe Harbor (EU/US)

As explained in the previous section, to keep information flowing between the European Union and the United States, the US Department of Commerce negotiated Safe Harbor (Commerce, US Deparment of 2010) provisions to allow certain companies to transfer information if certain requirements are met. Basically, this is a process that allows US companies to comply with the EU data protection directive.

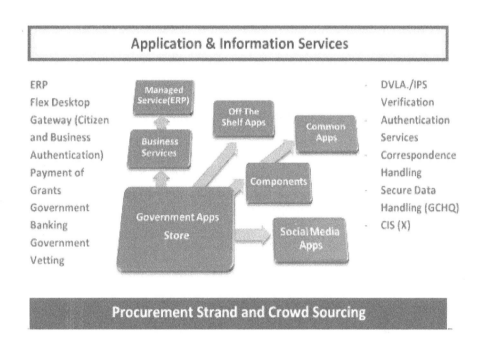

Figure 12 Application Store delivered in G-Cloud

In order to do this the company must adhere to seven principles:

- Notice: Inform affected individuals that data are being collected and how they are to be used.

- Choice: Permit individuals to opt-out from having data about them being collected and transferred.

- Onward Transfer: data transfer can be done only to other organizations that follow adequate data protection principles.

- Access: Individuals must be able to access the information about them and be able to correct or delete it if the information is inaccurate.

- Security: Take care of the data transfer to other organizations.

- Data Integrity: Have security measures to prevent loss and ensure data integrity.

- Enforcement: There must be effective means of enforcing these rules.

There should be an annual re-certification. It can perform a self-assessment to verify that complies (for this reason is subject of criticism) or get a third party to verify it. Some cloud providers offer geographic limits, so the data are only stored or processed in the countries requested by the customer

3.13.12 Apps.gov / FISMA

The Federal Information Security Management Act of 2002 FISMA recognizes the importance of information security and requires the head of each US agency to implement policies and procedures to cost-effectively reduce information technology security risks to an acceptable level.

It also requires sensitive data to stay within the US. Most of the cloud vendors are becoming certified against FISMA in order to be able to operate US government services. The idea is to establish standards for security and applications in order to make it easy for the US government to use cloud services. Google Apps for Government received FISMA certification in July 2010. There is a list of US Federal government-approved software at www.apps.gov, including cloud computing services and social media applications certified for federal government use. A similar model could be implemented by or for public organizations in Europe.

3.13.13 App Stores and Services Catalogues

The use of application stores and service catalogues is something that is not directly associated with cloud computing models, but will soon be used in these models as a simple way of offering services.

In this way customers can choose services and re-use them quickly when needed. The aim is to re-use as much as possible, having a set of services and applications that are generic enough to be used by different organizations and that have been successfully implemented and used by other organizations.

In spite of the many resources and technologies available to public organizations, many challenges have been encountered in developing and implementing e-government systems. According to Pockharel and Park, cloud computing and related technologies can address some of the traditional challenges (Park 2009). A good example is the UK G-Cloud initiative, where an app store will be created with a service catalogue of standard services that could be used by different government organizations. Figure 3 shows the service catalogue proposed for the UK G-Cloud. Figure 4 shows the app store delivery model for the UK G-Cloud. (Martin Bellamy 2011)

Applications and services can be provided by governmental organizations, by different vendors, or even by the public and can be added to the existing ones, bringing new functionality or extra services. The applications and services should be controlled by a specific body (normally part of the government that will use them) that will review them to ensure they meet the required standards.

3.13.14 GovCloud implementation examples

- o A good example of how providers are starting to create services specifically for government use is Amazon GovCloud for the US. The implementation is such that that the infrastructure is not shared with other non-government customers; providing machine, network and data isolation. It is also assigned to Amazon's US region, ensuring data do not leave the US and that the service complies with FISMA moderated controls. It is used by US agencies such as NASA for image processing using massive parallel computation on EC2, the US Treasury and USDA. A similar example is the Microsoft standards-based open data initiative called the Open Government Data Initiative (OGDI) that uses the Windows Azure platform to make it easier to publish and use a wide variety of public data from US government agencies (Mutavdzi 2010).
- o Other specific implementations by government organizations are:
- o UK: G Cloud (UK Government Cloud Strategy n.d.)
- o European Union: EuroCloud

o   Canada: Canada Cloud Computing (Canada Cloud Strategy n.d.)
o   Japan: Kasumigaseki Cloud (Kasumigaseki Japan Cloud Strategy n.d.)
o   For the US Government some case studies are described in the report from CIO (Kundra 2010), some of the solutions are:
o   GSA: Federal Cloud Computing Initiative – Apps.gov
o   Federal Chief Information Officer's Council: Data.gov & IT Dashboard
o   Energy: Magellan
o   Department of Defense (United States Army) - Army Experience Center
o   Department of Defense (Defense Information Systems Agency) - Rapid Access Computing Environment, Forge.mil
o   Department of Defense (United States Air Force) - Personnel Services Delivery Transformation
o   Department of Energy - Cloud Migration
o   Department of Health and Human Services - Supporting Electronic Health Records
o   Department of the Interior / General services administration – Agency wide E-mail
o   General Services Administration (Office of Citizen Services) - USA.gov
o   General Services Administration - Agency-wide E-mail
o   NASA-National Aeronautics and Space Administration (Ames Research Center) - World-Wide Telescope; (Jet Propulsion Laboratory) - Be A Martian, the Enterprise Data Center Strategy and Nebula
o   Social Security Administration - Online Answers Knowledgebase
o   Federal Labor Relations Authority - Case Management System
o   Recovery Accountability and Transparency Board - Recovery.gov Cloud Computing Migration

3.13.15 Moving public Information systems to the cloud

Some points to take into account when moving or creating Information Systems in cloud environments in public organisations are:

- Develop a cost competitive analysis of the internal costs vs. cloud costs.

- Define clearly the position towards our customers: will we permit to our customers to directly go to the cloud providers? Can we prevent them from doing it?
- When defining the systems in the cloud we should stress the splitting of responsibilities, workflows, SLAs and support.
- Make sure the migration process is well defined, so that business continuity is guaranteed.
- Launch cloud pilots and low risk service experiences, specially taking into account the data classification level, re-evaluating periodically. They will be very useful to fine-tune longer term strategy and procurement.

A suitable approach for some public organisations is:

- Create an inventory based on the existing services and applications.
- Develop a risk assessment for services and applications that will be moved to the cloud.
- Classify them and establish profiles facilitating the choice of the cloud solution that would be suitable (if any).

These topics should help to understand the opportunities and risks in order to define the long term strategy and how the service catalogue of public organisations will be shaped regarding to the balance of internal and cloud services.

3.13.16 Conclusion

The savings from implementing cloud computing will come by finding economies of scale in ICT and sharing resources between different public organizations. The decision to go for cloud solutions should be taken from a strategic point of view, taking into account long-term strategies and technologies. There should always be an exit strategy, in case it should become necessary to move services in-house or to a different provider.

Considering the different cloud models and deployment strategies, there is not a clear conclusion that any one model is most appropriate and in most cases a combination of them, one having greater prevalence is likely to be appropriate. The community model is especially interesting for public organizations. Sharing resources implies fewer and bigger data centres as is happening now in the private sector. There will be new government services from different cloud providers, like Govcloud from Amazon for Europe. It is important that clear standards and strategies are defined at the highest possible level for outsourcing and use of cloud services. Organizations must make sure they have enough technical expertise to evaluate and manage the solution. Enterprise architects and contract managers with the ability to understand complex pricing plans and technologies will be required. Procurement procedures will need to evolve to deal with cloud utility services.

The main indirect benefits of the use of cloud services in public organizations will come from the use of app stores and social media. The first will permit re-use of software and services, mainly when using SaaS and PaaS, permitting rapid deployment of new functionality. The use of social media and collaboration directly with users could permit a new paradigm in the way the public services are used by the public, allowing users to add and manipulate data and even applications that will use the data, shifting the power of manipulating and managing data to users directly.

In order to accomplish this change successfully it is very important that public bodies work together with providers (Jeffery 2009) defining proper standards and services that met the requirements of public bodies. Examples of this are starting to happen in countries like the UK and USA. An especially in time of cost reduction and austerity, moving more services and applications to cloud models seems very attractive, but this could be traumatic if not done properly.

However, if done with care, it could reduce cost, permit public organizations to re-focus their efforts, add new functionality and provide a better service for both the public organization and citizens.

3.14   Big-Open Data: Big data in public organizations

The use analytics in big datasets by private organisations like Facebook or Google is increasing at the same pace as the size of the datasets. But despite the same data volume grow in governmental organisations running public services the use of these datasets is not increasing at the same pace. It is true that open data has emerged from public and government organisations, but this is not happening for big data and how this is processed. In this article we explore how big data is used by public organisations and why the use of big data is not so extended on these organizations. The following article studies the challenges and opportunities that public organizations have in order to leverage from the huge amount of data that they manage and to improve the capability to forecast and improve the speed and accuracy in the decision-making for providing better public services.

3.14.1 Introduction

Governments have used analytics and business intelligence with their datasets for a long time, but recently the volume of these data sets have increased, in some cases becoming a problem instead of being part of a solution. The tools used until now for business intelligence are not always valid for these new datasets. Most governmental organisations lack the computational power, data storage and personnel needed to make use of Big Data (expanding volume of high velocity, complex and diverse types of data (Steven A. Mills 2012)). Also in some cases datasets are not properly used or understood, decisions are not based on quality data, or the responses based on data arrive too late to take the decisions within an appropriate timeline.

This article explains the impact and benefits for public organisations of big data and the issues of why governments are slow to adopt it. We describe the approaches to big data and real-time trends from business analytics. The existing literature does not cover this in detail, especially for governmental organisations. Section 1 of the paper is the introduction. In the section 2 we talk about what makes big data in public sector and the reasons why its use has not been extended to public organisations. In section 3 we give a few examples of big data in public organisations, focusing in health sector. Sections 4 and 5 describe the opportunities and challenges of big data for public sector finishing with the relationship between big data and open data for public sector and conclusions.

3.14.2 Big data in the public sector

3.14.2.1 *What makes big data in the public sector?*

The term big data is used for datasets with increasing volume (amount of data), velocity (speed of data in and out), and variety (range of data types and sources). In cases like Google, Facebook or other companies such as Walmart it is easy to recognise these, but what about public sector and governments?

The public sector has been using datasets in business intelligence and analytics for a long time. These datasets have grown but in most cases their analytical use has not grown at the same pace as in other organisations (Olavsrud 2012). Structured data (such as transactional business data, scientific research, and web interaction data) and unstructured data (such as reports, video, images) have grown in the governmental organisations at an unprecedented pace. But this data is not always used for taking strategic decisions as in private companies.

One factor that could dramatically increase the volume of data and the need to process it is what is called the Internet of Things (Sundmaeker, et al. 2010) and Machine-to-Machine (M2M) communications (Bourgeau, Chaouchi and Kirci 2013). All types of devices and objects will be able to use sensors to send data about their environment. An example is a device such as a smartphone that has a specific sensor for health monitoring that can send data instantly about the health of the owner.

3.14.2.2   Why big data is not used more in public organisations?
This has not been due to the lack of transactions and data that can be collected in public organisations, but to different factors. The first one is the fact that the technologies used to store and process the data have not been able to cope with the increase in data volume growth. Another factor is not having the specialised "Data Scientist" personnel (Vangelova 2012), professionals that are able to analyse the huge amount of data using this new set of tools. Associated with this factor is the issue of ownership of the data by the different business areas and IT. The responsibilities of both business and IT departments towards the use of that data are not always clear.

An additional factor is the system classification and categorisation of the data, especially for systems where there are large amount of text or non-structured information such as health data. A good ontology and set of reference terms could be the difference between having datasets that can be used to acquire knowledge or raw data that can merely be retrieved. The "Medical dictionary of regulatory activities" (MedDRA (International Conference on Harmonisation of Technical Requirements for Registration of Pharmaceuticals for Human Use (ICH) 2013)) by the International Federation of Pharmaceutical Manufacturers and Associations (IFPMA) or "EU Telematics Controlled Terms" (EUTCT (European Medecines Agency (EMA) 2011)) by EMA are examples of these systems.

3.14.3   Examples of Big Data in the public sector
We describe here some examples of the use of big data by government organizations in order to illustrate possible uses in public sector, especially in health segment.

3.14.3.1   Big data research and development initiative

Six US Federal departments and agencies (Policy 2012) are investing 200 million dollars to improve the tools and techniques needed to access, organize, and glean discoveries from huge volumes of digital data for scientific discovery, environmental and biomedical research, education, and national security. One of the projects inside this initiative is the 1,000 genomes data project available on the cloud and lead by the National Institute of Health. It is the world's largest set of data (200 Terabytes) on human genetic variation. It is freely available on the Amazon Web Services (AWS) cloud, where researchers only pay for the computing services that they use.

3.14.3.2   Surveillance and Security

The US Department of Energy National Lab uses TerraEchos (IBM Software 2012) as a solution to detect, classify, locate and track potential threats to secure its perimeters and border areas. The system captures and analyses vast amount of data in real time in order to detect potential threats. The solution continuously consumes and analyse digital acoustic data to extract meaningful intelligence, for example distinguishing between sounds of an animal versus a trespasser. The solution has been implemented using TerraEchos and IBM technology that permits analyse and correlate the data in real-time.

3.14.3.3   Health initiatives

Big data analytics in government health agencies (Bertolucci 2012) could allow organisations to target studies on improving pharmacovigilance, getting more information about specific diseases, and improve data-driven clinical support systems that could help prevent illnesses and personalise health advice. Medical devices, mobile Internet and the Internet of Things (Sundmaeker, et al. 2010) will connect together devices where sensors can follow the patient and devices permitting real-time prompt warnings to be sent and could help to identify health issues earlier (Mena, et al. 2013). Other benefit from the use of analytics in health care is reducing readmission rates by better monitoring of in-home aftercare. The concept of evidence-based medicine is becoming more common, where treatment decisions for patients are made based on the best scientific evidence available. The University of Ontario (UOIT) uses medical monitoring streams analytic software capable of managing petabytes of streaming data to detect infections in premature infants up to 24 hours before they exhibit symptoms (IBM n.d.).

Currently there are many initiatives in both private and public sectors to use big data for research in infectious diseases and cancer. An example is the use of the IBM Watson computer for processing Sloan-Kettering clinical datasets for cancer research (Horowitz 2012) uses natural-language processing (NLP) capabilities to interpret queries from doctors in unstructured documents, such as admittance records, doctors' notes, research findings and journal articles. AM Biotechnologies is using Cloud High Performance computing HPC to analyze DNA sequence to create unique aptamer compounds (Mark Shumbera 2012) to develop improved therapeutics for many medical conditions and diseases. And Google Flu Trends is a good example based on search activity of the forecast of influenza trend. Examples in health organisations are pharmacovigilance or clinical trial systems. Janus project, used by the US Food and Drug Administration's FDA or EudraCT by the European Medicines Agency (EMA) use past clinical trial data to enable to do better clinical trials in the future.

3.14.4   Big Data Opportunities for the Public Sector

3.14.4.1   Public customer services improvement

Probably the biggest benefit of big data is that it can be used to improve service levels of public services. Benefits include areas such as personalisation of services that provide more relevant information, to reducing the time needed to providing those services thanks to better knowledge of how the services are provided. This can be achieved with reliable predictive analytics, in some cases building models that show how they will evolve in the future based on the data from day-to-day operations from public services. This will allow what is known as evidence-based policy making. In the same way that big private companies like Amazon personalise their website based on the preferences of the customer, governmental organisations can personalise their health services to offer specific services based on health information such as risk factors. This could also be used to apply benefits and other services to citizens that are entitled to, but fail to claim them.

3.14.4.2   Innovation and research

One of the main opportunities is the possibility of finding hidden patterns and correlations in huge datasets. This does not mean that specialised personnel will not be needed. As has been stated before, it will be extremely important to have people that know the tools and what to look for. Using analytics to detect trends in order to forecast with a high degree of precision can help research and decision-making in certain areas when dealing with very critical or complex systems. An example is the use in pharmacovigilance, where drug adverse reaction reports are used to identify new information about hazards associated with medicines and preventing harm to patients in the future, or having a better idea of how diseases could spread using geodata and people behaviour data.

3.14.4.3   Sharing and cost reduction

Sharing and linking datasets can provide to governmental organisations knowledge through proper analytics tools that could help to improve the quality of public services and improve research in health, energy or environmental areas. This knowledge can help to improve efficiency, productivity and find cost savings. There are as well benefits from the point of view of not having to get, treat, store and maintain duplicate data from public services, with the reduction in costs. In some cases even the same agency or department request the same information twice for different processes creating a problem of inconsistency and quality of data. As an example, in the case of healthcare, data from different sources (clinical data, patient behaviour, pharmaceutical research) can be combined to get through analytics more information to improve decisions.

3.14.4.4   Improving control and reducing fraud

Big data analytics could help public organisations improve the visibility, control and auditing of the services they provide. This information can be made public (open data), improving as well the transparency of how the services are managed by exposing some key performance indicators (KPIs) such as productivity, helping the organisations to identify areas of underperformance and transferring resources to areas where they are most needed. This could allow those responsible to act faster based on this knowledge, and can reduce fraud and error by using better algorithms where more data is taken into account, not only from public organisations but from other sources such as social media. Also, as financial services do real-time checks for fraudulent transactions, public administration could use similar systems to avoid fraud when dealing with public funds, grants and benefits.

3.14.5   Challenges of Big Data in public sector

3.14.5.1   Data protection and Privacy

One of the main issues for governmental organisations is who owns the data and how it is used. This is clearer for certain organisations, but for other public organisations like national health systems and hospitals the collection and use of this type of data is not always defined.

Also there is a big concern with the privacy of individuals and their desire not to be tracked. Governmental organisations in particular need to be careful with this issue and not to rely on using synthetic or anonymised data in order to solve problems (Yiu 2012). In some cases the datasets are anonymised before being processed, but it has been demonstrated that this does not always assure the privacy of the data. It has been proven several times that governmental data, even after identifiers are removed, that when geographic or demographic data are still available, it can be used to match fields in the released data to other databases in order to identify an individual (Machanavajjhala and Reiter 2012). There are also risks related to the ethical and moral use of these powerful tools. An ethical code and proper controls should be defined to avoid improper use.

3.14.5.2   Infrastructure Architecture Technologies Requirements

One of the big challenges for governmental organisations is the change of the infrastructure-architected approach that is needed in their IT systems and datacentres. It is normal that datasets outgrown their current management tools. Until now the approach in their datacentres was more processor focused, but now it is changing to a focus on I/O, data storage and management. In some cases having a generic ICT infrastructure approach where most systems with similar requirements run without problems is not enough (Ranganathan and Chang 2012). This is linked to the need to improve the software for data acquisition, processing and analysis. Also, change the current data architecture, as well as the need for staff that are specialized in big data makes it difficult to deal with big data, particularly for agencies or organizations that, due to their size have insufficient resources.

Process of big data requires exceptional ICT infrastructure to efficiently process the quantity of data required in the expected times. The main characteristics of the ICT infrastructure used for big data are commonly high system performance, real-time processing, low cost and the use of commodity infrastructure. But some of these are in conflict; an example is the use of data in memory (expensive) when possible instead of having data in SATA disk (cheap). Some governmental organisations are looking into cloud solutions or hybrid solutions (Diez and Silva 2013) for benefits such as scalability, elasticity, self-provisioning and pay-as-you-go charging models. Cloud solutions permit to use these services without the initial capital expenditure needed for the infrastructure. One possible solution is sharing resources between different agencies (Zhang, Big Services Era: Global

Trends of Cloud Computing and Big Data 2012), so the investment on these technologies and the benefits of the use is also shared. In order to achieve this goal the standardisation of systems and having clear standards for data sharing are key issues. The datasets can be used by different systems, especially if data wants to be shared between different governmental organisations. All this should happen without bringing down the security aspect that requires storage and manipulation of the data, mostly personal and in some cases extremely sensitive.

3.14.5.3   Software Tools

For software tools we need to take into consideration how the data is stored, how it is handled and how it is analysed. Regarding the storage system, two main new approaches are parallel DBMS (such as IBM Netezza Data warehouse, Vertica, VoltDB or SAP Hana) that are based on massive parallel processing MPP architectures and NoSQL systems (such as Hadoop/Hbase, Cassandra, Amazon SimpleDB) that are less restricted than standard RDBMS to improve performance. For data handling, the main strategy is divide and conquer, implemented by map/reduce (Humbetov 2012), being the data divided and processed in parallel. Examples are Apache Pig (Mehine 2011) and Dryad (Isard, et al. 2007). The last stage is that of Knowledge Discovery in Databases "KDD", where the data is analysed, with products such as GNU R, SAS, Hive or Apache Mahout.

Many people associate open source tools like Apache Hadoop and Map/Reduce when talking about big data. But these types of tools are not always the solution, especially for medium and small governmental organisations. We need to take into account that these frameworks are still not mature enough and under constant progress and require large amount of development, configuration and IT expert resources (Madden 2012). It will be necessary in most of the cases to change the existing software interfaces and algorithms to cope with these volumes. Most business analytics software companies (such as Netezza, Teradata or Greenplum) offer different solutions to deal with big data, at least to deal with multiple petabytes, enough for most government agencies.

Sometimes massively parallel-processing (MPP) technologies are used, for example the use of MPP relational databases. This is another approach to distribute query processing. It has things in common with Map/Reduce such as the data processing is distributed across computer nodes, processing of data in each node and reassembling the results to produce a final set. But in the case of

MPP, very expensive and specialized hardware is used to get higher performance instead of using clusters of commodity servers with cheaper hardware. This makes them less scalable as the Map/Reduce model. But it has some advantages such as the possibility of using SQL (Structure Query Language) declarative queries directly instead of using Java directly or abstraction layers such as Hive. The SQL queries are usually know by a higher number of IT and non IT specialist, easier to use and more productive than the jobs created for Map/Reduce. Some vendors such as HortonWorks and Microsoft are recently trying to unify both worlds such as in Windows Azure HDInsight Service, a Microsoft Hadoop offering in Windows Azure with integration for SQL Server business intelligence products (Microsoft 2013).

So governmental organisations should base their decision on their data architecture and what tool will provide their requirements, looking different types of implementation from in-house solutions to cloud solutions such as Continuity.

3.14.5.4   Data quality and format

Another challenge is related to the quality of data in existing datasets. In some cases it is referred to as the fourth "V" for veracity (Steven A. Mills 2012), referring to data quality. Government data quality has improved during the last years thanks to the use of business intelligence and need for transparency in public organisations. But if datasets will be brought together these should be of high quality, or at least of the same quality levels. Not only are the data owners responsible for the quality of their data but also the people who bring the datasets together should verify the traceability and justification of those data-based decisions.

Other characteristics to take into account on top of veracity are validity and volatility. For validity we mean if the data is correct and accurate for the intended usage. Volatility refers to the period that we will need to store the data. This will imply that clear rules are established about the live-cycle of the data, including retention requirements and policies, and for each type of data. These rules should cover data creation, storage, processing and later archiving or deletion when no longer is needed. For this, public organisations must not only meet the analytical requirements but legal and regulatory requirements.

Clear, open and standard data formats are key to the success of big data for public organisations. And sometimes are these public organisations that should take the lead in the definition, adoption and promotion of those standards. Open

Application programming interfaces (APIs) should follow, particularly when dealing with open data and exchange of data between different public organisations. An example of these formats is the effort by OASIS Business-Centric Methodology Technical Committee (Borras, et al. 2013) to have standards for data interchange in medical devices, using definitions for templates and device taxonomy of ANSI/CEA-721. This will provide medical device manufacturers the possibility of gather, storing, interchange and analysing information. It is key to move from proprietary formats to open ones, and this is not always easy as proprietary standards provided a company with a mechanism to hold more tightly onto their customers. But a complete change from proprietary standards and formats to open ones will not be easy. A proposed approach is to take an incremental structure implementation of open formats.

Reference data standards will enable to easily integrate information from different sources, internal and external to the organisation, permitting to increase the quality, scope and accuracy of the analytics. Until now most of the information was structure and classified taking into account the requirements of the application that was made for, creating silos, sometimes internally into the organisation, but always externally. We were not capturing and storing data thinking into the future, in how that data could be used by other systems. Now, we should look beyond the boundaries of the organisation, using reference data standards to map and interpret data from different systems to increase the scope of the domain and improving the analytics applied to those systems.

3.14.5.5   *Business and ICT alignment*

As we said before, one of the main challenges is ownership of the data and the alignment between business and ICT. Who is responsible of using the data and how it should be used, what questions should be asked, what information should be stored and how it should be captured. In some cases the success will depend on the ability and wishes of the organisation to redesign the business processes to get the required information. ICT departments will also need to replace classic and well-established information architectures for new ones more focused on data that allows it to be manipulated properly. All this will be a challenge for governmental organisations as there is also a high pressure for costs reduction. We need to take into account the return on investment. As Goldston (Goldston 2008) describes we must be sure of not spending money on measuring a problem rather than in solving it.

3.14.6   Opening the Big Data in Public Sector

3.14.6.1   *Big data and open data*

As was stated before, governmental organisations such as healthcare ones have huge amounts of data and much of it is not used. Making this information available to researchers, consumers and companies can lead to improvements in areas such as healthcare. But putting this vast amount of data available to everyone is not always easy. It is not practical to transfer these huge amounts of data and most of the time consumers and non-governmental organisations do not have the systems/tools/resources to manipulate it. There is currently a set of principles defined by the open government-working group (group 2007) to govern the use of open data. The main principles are:

- Data must be complete

- Data must be primary

- Data must be timely

- Data must be accessible

- Data must be machine processable

- Access must be non-discriminatory

- Data Formats must be non-proprietary

- Data must be license-free

- Compliance must be reviewable

The combination of both open data and big data will be key. Tools used to manipulate and analyse the big data owned by public organisations could, in some cases, be accessible by public and other partners to formulate their own queries.

In other initiatives the public or diverse organisations could add datasets or data to existing datasets in order to increase the quality of that data. An example is pharmacovigilance systems where the public could enter specific data, or where specific devices send data authorised by the users directly to these datasets to be analysed.

Other uses when opening data to the public and external organisations are crowd-sourcing and micro-work, where specific tasks that normally would be difficult to process by algorithms are done by people, being these tasks reimbursed or not. This has huge potential for dealing with big datasets, especially when datasets have unstructured or improperly classified data, like what happens in some health data such as pharmacovigilance records. An example of this type of platforms is Amazon Mechanical Turk.

3.14.7 Current open data initiatives

There are currently different open data initiatives for example data.gov or data.gov.uk (Government 2012). As well some specific initiatives such as the Held Data Initiative or healthdata.gov where information from the U.S. Department of Health and Human Services has been made public. These datasets include data from different US agencies, such as National Institutes of Health (NIH), the Centers for Medicare and Medicaid Services (CMS) and Centers for Disease Control and Prevention (CDC). The information includes databases of recent medical and scientific knowledge, consumer product and government spending data, and numerous other reports.

3.14.8 Conclusion

Big Data in governmental organisations should come from a clear and open policy where the justification and the strategy for big data are defined. In most cases this means that we can move from currently installed business analytics and datasets to systems that could cope with the new requirements. We should always take into account the privacy of the citizens. Respecting the taxpayers and citizens' rights and privacy should always be the primary concern when developing big data systems. One of the goals is to evolve from the concept of asking questions about the data to being informed through data analytics. We should not focus only on technology, but on how the processes are architected to extract knowledge faster. Processing and analysis must be organised and directed in a different way, where less manual intervention is needed for faster cycles and shorter processes.

Sharing infrastructure, datasets, staff and resources between governmental organisations should become the norm, not the exception. Consolidation can bring huge savings and open the possibility of using datasets that could not be used otherwise if those resources were not available. In order to achieve this, standards and reference data formats are crucial, and public organisations should lead by example.

Regarding staff, Data Scientists will be necessary in governmental organisations to get the most out of big data. External organisations and consultancy companies can help to deploy the new tools and systems, but people with knowledge of the organisation and of the toolsets will be the ones who could bring most value to big data. Specialised analytical and data teams should be appointed in different organisations. It will be important to train internal people with knowledge of the new analytical systems to get the best of the new tools. The people responsible for taking decisions and policymaking should take data-driven decisions, not based only on the results of the data and analytics, but in combination with their own and other perspectives to take the best decisions and policies for the citizens and taxpayers.

"Correctness is clearly the prime quality. If a system does not do what it is supposed to do, then everything else about it matters little."

[Bertrand Meyer]

4   Cloud Services Resilience and Reliability

When dealing with resilience, dependability and reliability one approach is to consider them at every level. Decomposing the system in small parts, reviewing them for each part, and later all together. There are two main issues with this approach, one with cloud environments as said before is that usually we do not know how really is implemented the system, because is proprietary technology. The second issue is related with the fact of the complexity of cloud environments, where different number of technologies is used. Examples of the complexity is the use of runtime environments like java, or the use of virtualization, where dependability with hypervisors is still being reviewed and is not so solid as more established operating systems, and all these needs to be put together. And in dependability complexity is a big enemy.

One of the main issues now with the use of cloud services is trust on the cloud provider. The main issue is that the providers do not offer enough information about what they really have in operation, mainly because this is their business advantage to the other providers and made them attackable by hackers. For most of the cloud services the contracts and SLAs are defined based on availability, and not always based on previous data, but on estimation based on the provider's criteria.

All the main concerns that apply to use of Internet or networks for CIs applies as well to the cloud services, because most of them are provided using interconnected datacentres over networks and most of cases the Internet, as well the access to these systems is done over internet. I will focus in the reliability, some pros and cons for each cloud model related to reliability are described in table 1, but other aspects should be covered in the use of cloud services for CIs, especially legal, regulatory compliance, response, recovery and security. Cloud services are here to stay, and will become a new utility, so why not to use it in the same way that most of CIs industries use other utilities like water or electricity supplies? There are two main differences, one is complexity associated with the cloud model that his higher than in other models, the second is the time that took to these utilities to become reliable, as we know it now, and basically all of them are now in a very mature stage. Even in these cases, for CIs there are systems to improve reliability and availability when these utilities fail, like electrical generators or water tanks for chemical plants with continuous processing. Table 13 shows the pros and cons in de different types of cloud implementations as well as who is usually managing the system. As we can see there is not a model that can solve all the main issues. The decision will depend on the type of requirements for each model and the security and privacy of the data will have relevance when taking the decision on what solution we should take.

Model	Public	Community	Private
Pros	.elasticity & absorb demand .Geographical distribution .Large pool .Low control	.medium to full control .common requirements	.governance .monitoring .Full control of solution .less prone to attacks
Cons	.monitoring is difficult .prone to attacks .issues related to Tenancy .Lack of governance	.trust on other members of community. .smaller pool than public	.small pool .elasticity & absorb demand .lack of geo-redundancy
Managed by	External provider	Oraganization/External	Organization

Table 5 Cloud models and reliability.

4.1   A new concept for Resilience and Reliability

We see that the traditional hardware fault models do not fit when used in cloud services. The interconnection is a crucial component of the system in cloud environments and a new virtualization layer is adding dependability of the hypervisors. As well, the normal reactive fault tolerance model is not appropriate. The 24/7 business availability implies that proactive fault tolerance is needed. The recovery time correlates to the system size, doing reactive fault tolerance inappropriate, as it does not scale accordingly. We see that although outages are rare, they are inevitable. This is something we all have to deal with when using any type of systems, and it applies to cloud systems also.

But hardware and software vendors are moving to a more proactive management of errors. There is hardware monitoring and a preventive reaction expected from software like IBM Predictive Failure Analysis (PFA) or the Intel Machine Check Architecture (MCA)

As described by Troger (Troger 2011) there are two points of view, the provider's and the customer's. In the Provider's point of view reliability, resilience and availability become another quality attribute. The focus is not so much in hardware but software, where new approaches are more affordable. There are new ideas for achieving scalable and reliable cloud centers, like leverage virtualization capabilities, dynamic monitoring and tracing, smart event correlation for anomaly detection or hardware failure prediction for x86 environments. At the customer side, the customer needs predictable scalability for minimal costs, application-driven cost optimization and as a minimum the same reliability as his local data center. But the customer gets a programming model for a black box. The customer needs to have independence of the vendor and standard monitoring for the status and control. The current dependability models for cloud computing as said before are not adequate, including the modeling approaches and the reactive fault tolerance.

4.2   How the reliability is achieved in the cloud

One very simple and easy way of calculating the reliability and try to find out the cost of the system for different implementations is to use the K-of-N approach based in Boolean logic and the serial and parallel cases. If we use a similar approach normally the cheaper solution having still high numbers in reliability will be using the parallel model, so having many components where the reliability of the component is not too big, but having a big number in parallel the reliability will increase. Basically most of the main vendors opt for having cheaper and less reliable components, but having them in parallel to provide speed and higher reliability.

In most cases we see implementations where instead of using big and very reliable supercomputers, cloud vendors use simple and cheap hardware but in big quantities, as an example is the use of storage. It is as well taken into account when we talk about price not only the purchase cost but also the maintenance and support costs.

Most of the providers, such as Microsoft (Marc Mercuri 2012) with Windows Azure offer some advice and patterns for resilience when designing applications that will work on their environments.

4.2.1   Regions and availability zones

Most of the big cloud providers (such as Amazon and Google) are organised in regions. These regions provide normally the same type of services. The region describes the geographic location where the resources are stored. A zone is an isolated location within a region that is independent of other zones in the same region. Each zone consists of one or more distinct data centers. The customer usually can choose in what region/zone is used, giving him control over where the data is stored and used.

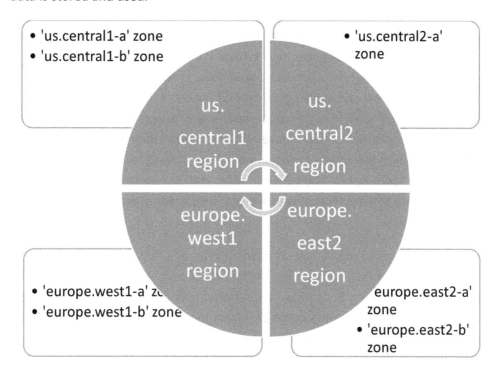

Figure 13 Google availability regions and zones example

Availability zones are designed to shield the customer infrastructure from physical harm, like hurricanes. If one data center is affected, the customer should be able to use another one by switching to another availability zone. Availability zones are very important in order to improve resilient and reliability when working with cloud vendors. Using traffic managers/load balancers (such as Amazon Elastic Load Balancer ELB) we can configure it to distribute the traffic evenly across one or more availability zones. We should make sure that we can replace the instances easily in case of losing instances or even losing an entire zone. We can get an almost unlimited supply of instances.

4.2.2   Designing resilience applications for cloud environments

Infrastructure literally moves into software engineering. Probably the most important factor when dealing with resilience in cloud environments is how to design the application/infrastructure for reliability. It is important for the architects and developers to understand resilience in cloud computing and apply it to their systems using different techniques such as spreading data across zones.

The resilience should be a property of the application as a whole, not only the infrastructure. This means that both operations and development teams work together to ensure that the applications could survive when parts of the network/cloud go down. Both teams should have a basic understanding of the vendors services cloud engineering. Software developers need to understand about the different ways to persist data in their vendor and how to make sure that the system will still working in case of issues. It is a good idea to share operational responsibility, as that is the fastest way to spread this information. A good example is Netflix's ChaosMonkey that randomly kills instances and services within the application to see how the system survives to random incidents. The development and operations teams must collaborate to ensure that the applications are sufficiently robust to withstand constant random outages without degrading.

When possible try to use as less as possible type and number of resources. The less resources we have, the less they will fail. When possible kill unused resources, not only to reduce cost but to have a cleaner environment. Use as many off-the-shelf components, and always preferably from the cloud vendor. Do not reinvent the wheel, and expend time on things that can add value instead.

Almost all vendors offer nowadays tools designed to improve the resilience and reliability of our systems. When possible we should use them (e.g. Amazon's CDN and Route53). Also there are open source tools that provide a reliable solution to common problems and can be used in the cloud vendor infrastructure using plug-ins. An example is Elasticsearh for distributed real-time search and analytics engine (basically a NoSQL-type Big Data solution).

4.2.3 Asynchronous communications

When possible, we should try to design our applications using cloud services to use asynchronous interactions. This will provide autonomy to that system, being more resilience in case of failure. An easy way of achieving this is with the use of queues when different elements interact. Other is the use of stateless web apps and the use of distributed cache at web-tier level.

4.2.4 Temporary faults

The most common way of handle faults is the use of timeouts, normally based on a specific timeframe when the expected response is not received in time or is not what is expected. Errors are generated based on the context where the failure have been produced and can be based in the impact of the error, the number of times this error has occurred or other parameters. But these faults can be permanent or what are considered temporary (normally less than a few seconds). It is important to deal with the temporary ones gracefully. This could be implemented in different ways and will depend on the type of application and fault, but it could imply that the application uses temporary queues, cache, or any other mechanism to queue the workload until the fault disappears and still processing request from the customers so it is transparent for the customer.

Different possibilities could be used to deal with these types of faults. The most used is to retry the operation again after waiting a specific time during a specific number of times. In some cases the retries can be done not at the same intervals of time, but in an exponential way, this is known as "exponential backoff", to avoid throttling. In most of the cases when using cloud services this could solve the issue. If after the specified number of times the fault persists an error can be raised or other way to deal with the fault should be used. The destination side can implement also mechanisms such as a circuit breaker patterns and throttling access for a specific period of time to avoid being saturated with so many requests. When the client exceed the number of allowed request within the time period the circuit breaker can include delays between requests until the request are in the permitted levels. Of course, there can be exceptions to the use of circuit breakers and throttling mechanisms in the form of white and black lists where specific clients with different SLAs could get higher levels of request per time unit.

When dealing with transient faults it is possible to send or receive the same data more than one times, we need to be sure that the programs are ready to manage this situations (Idempotency), so that receiving it multiple times or not in the expected order will not created errors or data corruption.

4.3   Private clouds

In the case of the private clouds, usually the customer does the design of the solution, and can control most of the supply chain involved in the service. This provides the possibility as well of implement services that could not be provided on other models like specific fail-safe or cluster mechanisms, as well as a closer management of the solution. It is possible as well to specify the system in detail and define SLAs for the service based on the requirements of the solutions. The solution can be tested thoroughly including all the components and a detailed business continuity plan can be created (except for geo-redundancy requirements). The main disadvantage of this model is that is more expensive than the others, due to the economies of scale of other models. It is true that not always the reliability and availability is better, because usually public or community models have bigger number of resources to serve peaks or DOS attacks. Other issue that can affect the reliability in some cases is the lack of geo-redundancy in business continuity.

In general, even if this model in theory could provide more reliability and availability due to the fact that can be customized, in reality and in long term, could not be similar to the redundancy or the availability offered by a public cloud provider. Private cloud models can be used for services where the public or community models cannot be used, and as a staged approach to the use of other models. Private model is a good candidate for CI organizations that would like to use cloud services, as the current public services offer solutions for non-critical services or average enterprise services. Some vendors, like VMWare with vcloud offers solutions for IaaS that permit migrate virtualize environments to internal clouds, and in a later stage move with minimum changes to a hybrid or public cloud.

4.4   Public clouds

The main benefits from this model come from the economy of scale factor, and the fact that the pool of resources is very large. The reliability is high due to the high number of hardware resources and the simplification of the infrastructure model. The control of the infrastructure is done by the vendor, as well as the business continuity strategy, that commonly is geo-located in different regions/countries. From the security and the monitoring point of view, the resources dedicated are higher.

But this homogenous and simplified model that improves economies of scale and lower costs is at the same time the main issue now for critical systems, mainly for the lack of offer of specific services that meet the demanded services. This will change in the future and more services will be offered to meet the requirements of more critical systems. Other possible problem is the lack of control in all the stages of the supply chain of the service and the fact that this could be an attractive target for hackers. The SLAs for these services are normally pre-defined by the provider, and there are not possibilities for negotiation, doing difficult to agree in specific reliability and availability figures needed for Critical systems. Unlike the private or community models where the datacentres can be implemented inside the premises of the customers, in the public are outside, and the reliability of the Internet or wan network needs to be taken into account. Other possible issue that could affect reliability for public cloud is the reputation fate sharing, where basically the issues with one of the tenants could affect to other tenants, an example is the case (Joshi, et al. 2009) where premises of a datacentre where closed and disconnected by the FBI due to investigation of criminal activities of one of the tenants.

4.5   Community clouds

This model is a combination of the two previous models, with the benefits and in some cases weaknesses of both, limiting the costs because a low cost entry barrier due to the fact that is divided between the different consumers, as well given more flexibility. In community clouds similar requirements of similar type of customers are met. This is particularly important for organizations with critical systems or critical infrastructures, where the public cloud model does not meet the requirements and reliability criteria requested by these systems. Similar organizations or government agencies can use this model for improve reliability and elasticity due to the increase in resources, and at the same time reduce costs due to the economies of scale. The users that can be part of this community cloud are restricted and normally well known, reducing the risks of having multi-tenancy.

Due to the common requirements and objectives the same utilization patterns could appear, reducing elasticity and flexibility in high peaks. This model could be a more attractive target for hackers/attackers, especially in community clouds for critical systems. Changes and improvements to the infrastructure and services needs to be agreed by the members, and is not always easy to find a consensus.

Other models like industrial cloud (Tomasz Wiktor Wlodarczyk 2009) are similar concepts to the community cloud, but with specialized collaboration concepts and are not described in detail in this work.

4.6   Cloud Service models

From the three main cloud models (Software as a Service SaaS, Platform as a Service PaaS, Infrastructure as a Service IaaS), SaaS is the one that offers less control to the customer, and this is linked usually to lack of control of the reliability of the system. In the other side, IaaS gives more direct control by the customer over the solution including the reliability of the system. In the same way, the private cloud offers more control of the solution to the customer than the community, hybrid or public.

4.7   Threats to reliability in cloud services

It is important when talking about reliability and availability differentiate between planned downtime and un-planned downtime. One of the advantages of using cloud systems is that if properly designed and due to the heavily use of virtualization the planned downtime is reduced to minimum, in some cases with providers offering 3 nines (99.9% or 8 hours per year). What is more important here is the un-planned downtime. Table 6 Outages in cloud providers shows some of the recent downtimes by main cloud providers (M, et al. 2010). As it happened with network providers when they started to offer new services, the reliability improves as the services mature. This happens because of the experience acquired by staff and proven processes as part of a better governance of the cloud services.

Service and Outage	Duration	Date
S3 outage: authentication service overload leading to unavailability	2 hours	15/2/08
S3 outage: Single bit error leading to gossip protocol blow-up	6–8 hours	20/7/08
AppEngine partial outage: programming error	5 hours	17/6/08
Gmail: site unavailable due to outage in contacts system	1.5 hours	14/5/09

Table 6 Outages in cloud providers

Part of the reliability is linked to the backup strategy of the provider, and the time to restore in case of an incidence, both for SQL and NoSQL data sets. Based on the business continuity requirements, the location of this replica could be with the same cloud provider, in the same data center, in the same No SQL data store, reside in a different data center, a different cloud provider and/or a different variant of NoSQL data store. The decision will be based on the workload service and any related regulatory compliance considerations.

Security would be as well paramount for reliability. Other aspect is the monitoring of the systems components and the systems as a whole, specially the proactive monitoring and capacity planning. The threats will depend on what assets will be moved to the cloud services, if are going to be specific processes or data or functions that currently are done by internal processes (CSA 2009). It helps to do a risk assessment on the reliability for the assets that will be moved to the cloud, and the impact of the Critical Infrastructure if the reliability is impacted. As described in the previous sections, the threats can be different depending of the type of cloud that will be used.

Cloud computing threats that could affect the reliability of the service are:

- Bad use by other tenants, in some cases being even hackers or attackers to the target systems. It is easy to attack from the inside. As well the reputation fate sharing, where issues of one tenant could affect the rest.
- Use of shared resources/technologies like the use of virtualization, one bug could affect to all systems even if the Operating systems where are running are different.
- Attractive targets for attackers and hackers due to the high number of tenants and importance of these services in the case of CIs.
- Lack of control over all the supply chain of components that are part of the service, where in some cases even the provider does not have control as he is using other services from other providers.

There are some initiatives in order to help to minimize the risks and assure reliability for cloud environment, like the CSA Guidance, the Common Assurance Maturity Model (CAMM) or the Consensus assessment, but are focused mainly in the security aspects of the cloud services.

4.7.1   Automation

Automation is a key feature of cloud services. Also it is a way of making any cloud service more resilient, reducing the human error. It could be done in different areas of the process, but it is mostly used using scripting for deployment, testing and management. Automation could facilitate developers the testing and deployment in different environments (development, test, staging, acceptance, and production), assuring that the same version is deployed in all environments and that it has been properly tested. This also will reduce the time to deploy in prod of new functionality.

4.8   Security and Reliability/Dependability

Although most of the concerns with cloud computing are related to security (Trusting vendor's security model, customer inability to respond to audit findings, obtaining support for investigations, indirect administrator accountability, proprietary implementations can't be examined, Loss of physical control), currently there is probably a bigger risk that is not so obvious but can be even more dangerous, that is the reliability and dependability of these systems.

According to the Study "Critical Infrastructure in the Age of Ciberwar" (Stewart Baker 2010) two-thirds of those surveyed (76%) said their systems were connected to an IP network or the Internet. About half of those said the connection created system security issues that are not being addressed. Other challenges that can impact reliability and dependability are the risk of having a future with only a few huge cloud providers (attacks, multi-tenant error propagation), and the lack of visibility having multiple administrative domains.

4.9   Design for Operations

It is particularly important for the resilience of a cloud system to take into account how the system will be working during the operation phase and take into account the main operation aspects (monitoring, event management, establish a health model, get telemetry information) during the design of the system. Information such as the health status of an application should be captured and processed in order to permit the self-healing of services (e.g. triggering a reboot or reimaging of a service to failing over to a different internal data or service provider). This should be more than a up/down view. Having a health model permits to know when a system could fail based on different criteria that will be monitored. This information could be obtained using active monitoring agents or provided by the application itself through health interfaces. Using interfaces based on existing mechanisms permits to be monitored not only by automated monitoring systems but for administrators and if needed developers as well with minimum effort. This provides also more visibility of the system in environments where it is not always possible to access this information through other interfaces (such as installing a monitoring agent into the system where the application is running).

4.10   Main interdependency risks and cloud-computing interaction

So what are the main interactions and risks of cloud computing systems when used in Critical systems and Critical infrastructures? We will describe some of the risks and the inter-dependencies that the use of cloud-computing systems.

4.10.1   Bugs in Large Distributed systems

One of the risks is the error on the very large-scale distributed systems. Especially if these errors do not appear in smaller "tests" environments, or cannot easily be reproduced without the intervention of large-scale systems. Both Critical Infrastructure systems and cloud systems are usually very large systems, being both a clear candidate for this type of errors due to the lack of testing environments that could reproduce production systems.

4.10.2 Geographic location of Cloud-computing Datacenters and Nodes

The same principle explained by T. Gyle Lewis (Lewis 2006) with the Internet nodes geolocation could be applied to the cloud provider nodes, especially when we are using different providers, and some of them have their facilities located in the same geographical area. Other risk associated to the location of the nodes is the use that the governments could have of these facilities. In the case of China or USA if they decide to take advantage of these cloud vendors in cases where national security is affected and how other countries could be affected with these decisions. Examples like the interaction of China Government with the Internet facilities or some providers like Google.

In a recent study (Stewart Baker 2010) the United States was seen as the most worrisome potential aggressor by large majorities of executives in countries where broader suspicions of U.S. motives are common—China (89%), Brazil (76%), Spain (67%), Mexico (65%) and Russia (61%). But even in a traditional U.S. ally like Germany, 45% named it the top concern, while only 34% named China, even though Germany's government has publicly criticized China for conducting computer network intelligence operations on key national assets.

We should take into account the physical, geographical and environmental characteristics of the cloud computing services and their dependencies also in public infrastructure and public services.

4.10.3 Connectivity (private networks or Internet)

Other important factor is the network connectivity, as most of the cloud services rely on Internet or other type of network connection. Most of the current networks, and specially Internet are highly resilient, but still are cases where the connectivity is not possible for different causes (downtime of providers, government restriction, damage to cables, etc...). Both the impact of downtime and latency should be taken into account when designing services that use cloud providers/technologies. It should be considered not only the connectivity to the datacenters that offer the cloud solution, but also the connectivity of these datacenters to other services they are relying on when possible.

4.10.4   Reputation Fate Sharing

This risk is explained by M. Armbrust (Michael Armbrust Feb 2009). In this case one customer's bad behaviour can affect the reputation of others using the same cloud provider. It can be affected in different ways, like blacklisting of EC2 IP addresses by spam prevention services. Another legal issue could be the transfer of legal liability where cloud-computing providers would want the customers to be liable instead of them. In March 2009, the FBI raided two floors of a Dallas datacentre (Miller 2009) and 'pulled the plug' on all clients web servers because a company whose services were hosted there was being investigated for possible criminal activity, but other 50 companies hosted in the same facility suffered days of unexpected downtime, and some went out of business.

4.10.5   Reliability Advantages/Disadvantages of Cloud computing

The main advantages and disadvantages of cloud computing regarding to resilience, dependability and reliability are described in Table 7 Advantages and disadvantages of using cloud systems.

There are more advantages and disadvantages that will be found in the future, as more information and more uses of these services are discovered. Other risks not related to reliability needs to be solved as well, like the ones related to property of the data. The president of the Microsoft Servers and tools business division responded to the journalist that Microsoft would move data held in EU from the Dublin to USA datacentre if this was requested by the US Department of Homeland Security (Patriot Act), and then hand it over. This has great impact from the point of view of Data protection in EU.

Advantages	Disadvantages
Low-Cost solution in some cases (Disaster Recovery and Data Storage Solutions), providing reliability at lower cost that other solutions.	Lack of physical control of where is the data and the processing, including the data and processing segregation.
Rapid Re-Constitution of Services	Quality of service guarantees
Greater Resiliency	Lack of standards / interoperability. A set of standards and/or interfaces have not yet been defined, risk of vendor lock-in.
Data Fragmentation and Dispersal	Possibility for massive outages
Parallel batch processing. using hundreds of computers for a short time costs the same as using a few computers for a long time. [9]	Attraction to hackers (high value target) Cloud providers not only provide highly visible targets for attackers but increases the risk of common mode outages affecting a large number of systems
Capital expenditure is minimized (lower entry barriers). The elimination of an up-front commitment by Cloud users, thereby allowing companies to start small, and increase hardware resources only when	Data Loss (difficult to impose availability constrains and backup and restore procedures), and recover Data Leakage (data centers outside customer firewalls and control)

needed. [9]	Data mistakenly changed due to transformation
Quality (great economy of scale and specialization, rigorous processes and procedures to maximize up-time and performance)	- Loss of Service - Service termination (provider insolvency) - Service interruption - Partial service interruption
Flexibility (easier to roll out new services, faster time to market)	Lock-in to one vendor (lack of standardization, too much effort to migrate)
Plan for provisioning. No need of doing a detailed capacity planning.	Investigating inappropriate or illegal activity may be impossible. Providers may not provide the cause of outages or other detailed design
Focus on core activities (reduces effort and administration that is required by the corporate ICT department)	Loss of reputation (if the provider can not guarantee the service)

Table 7 Advantages and disadvantages of using cloud systems

4.11   Fault Tolerance in Cloud computing

There are different ways to improve the fault tolerance in cloud computing scenarios. These are normally based on the way the replication of components is done. Starting with multiple servers in the same cluster, where different hosts run replicas of the same application. This configuration will benefit of higher bandwidth and low latency that other fault tolerance scenarios, but has limited independence to failures. Other replication model is having multiple clusters within a data center, where the application replicas are deployed in different set of clusters within the same datacenter. This improves the failure independence because a single failure in one cluster cannot affect the application, but still affected when the failure is at datacenter level. Other possible model, the one used by most cloud vendors to provide replication is to use multiple data centers. In this case the application replicas are deployed in hosts of different datacenters. This model has more latency than the others and probably lower bandwidth, but it offers a higher level of failure independence.

In some cases, this last model is still considered as an issue, due to the fact that only one company is still responsible of the systems, and has been proven in some cases that failures affect to more than one zone (as in the case of Amazon). A solution to this could be the use of federated cloud services, but this type of solutions are difficult because it implies that different providers should work together. Cloud brokers and the cloud of clouds paradigm could help to solve this issue, but there are still some technical challenges when using different providers.

In some cases it is necessary for compliance or business continuity reasons to have on-premises redundancy. To ensure this, we should use cloud services that will work across multiple cloud types or private cloud-deployable solutions. This can be done at application or workload level.

At the same time, fault tolerance can be managed at the provider level, at the customer level, or by a combination of both the provider and the customer. At the customer level, it could detect mainly faults at application and virtual machine level. Other failures such as hardware are easy to detect at provider level.

Regarding the implementation of fault tolerance by cloud providers, some such as OpenNebula offer it at virtual machine level, permitting to use scripts or programs with each type of virtual machine failure. Basically it has sensors at virtual machine level to detect failures and permit to execute different scripts or programs based on the type of failure. It is more difficult to offer this services at hardware level and most do not offer it. Other fault tolerance method used by Microsfot Windows Azure and Amazon EC2 is the replication of VM. There is a replica of each VM so the failure is covered by its replica and managed by the customer.

"Today, most software exists, not to solve a problem, but to interface with other software."

[I. O. Angell]

5   State of the Art

5.1   Introduction

This chapter will present and review the most relevant proposals of the published ones in the literature so far for dependability and resilience assessment on the use of cloud computer for critical infrastructures and systems.

There are two main types of approaches for studying the reliability of a system, one that is focused more on the design phase and is usually more formal and mathematical. The other one is to focus in the execution phase, which is more practical and heuristic. Both are imperfect, and while the first one can provide conclusions about the system behaviour in a proposed environment, the second can give actual behaviour of the intended environment where the system will work. But each has his advantages and limitations, and can be combined to get better and more accurate results.

In this section we will review the characteristics that are desirable for any dependability and resilience proposal aimed to be used in a cloud environment. The main characteristics that will be reviewed are:

- Holistic/reductionist Approach: what is the focus of the model/framework. If has a holistic approach and deals with the system as a whole or is focused in finding dependability, resilience and reliability of a specific system part (like network or hardware). It is better if the system is reviewed from a holistic approach as issues in one part of the system (like how the systems manage memory of virtual machines) can affect the overall resilience of the system.
- Micro coverage: This means that the proposal can be used in models where the level of abstraction is low, but the level of detail is high, thus permitting the use of the framework for more detailed and specific scenarios.
- Macro coverage: This means that the proposal can be used in models where the level of abstraction is high, but the level of detail is low. These include normally combination of customer ICT systems and cloud vendors systems. Ideally the framework should combine both micro and macro models and being able to use them together to get better understanding

of the systems, and be able to use more detailed data when there is the possibility.

- Operational phase: can be used after the system has been released into production environment and is in execution. This will permit to enhance the framework once the system is operational, and act according to changes in the systems when systems are dynamic (like use of different cloud vendors)

- Automatic feedback-triggered actions: the system can use feedback from how is working in real time to execute different actions automatically, without manual intervention, like change to different service B if service A is not working at the expected reliability levels. This will provide the framework of a way to act directly into the system based on the information from the current systems, giving the possibility of improve the resilience of the system once it is in operation.

- Multiple-source monitoring: The system gets information from different sources, some of them validated by authorities to obtain monitoring values that can be used for the calculation of the reliability values. This is linked to the measured perceived reliability: As defined by David Zeitler (Zeitler 1991) reliability can be related to perceived failures as opposed to what is considered actual failures by the cloud provider. Especially when the service relies on different systems. In this case the user or client is not satisfied with the operation of the system and it is considered unreliable. It would be ideal to detect and minimize all failures including user perceived failures. For this is very important to have a view of the system from the point of view of the final client and take all the subsystems and networks into account. The benefit for the framework is that having multiples sources of information will improve the quality of data, especially if this data needs to be used for taking automatic actions.

- Automated Service Level Agreement (SLA) checking: Using an automatic SLA system to obtain and check the SLA values to confirm that are within the agreement and if not take automatic actions, like the web service level agreement for web services WSLA or the WS-Agreement proposed by the GRAAP Working Group (Andrieux, et al. 2007) in the Open Grid Forum. This will imply that the framework have some SLAs and will automatically get information and values of indicators for these SLAs, improving the definition of what will be measured in the framework and the time to response.

- Recovery/dependability Means: mechanism used by the model/Framework to avoid faults to happen or to become failures. Depending on the type of model, the benefits can be different for the framework. There are the fault tolerance techniques (Fault prevention and removal) and fault tolerance techniques (Fault forecasting and tolerance):
  - o Fault Prevention (FP): Usually in design phase, to avoid faults in the system.
  - o Fault/Failure forecasting (FF): Monitoring data to forecast an upcoming failure. Some techniques like load prediction.
  - o Fault removal (FR): Make faults disappear before fault tolerance becoming relevant. An example is corrective maintenance.
  - o Fault tolerance (FT): Ability of a system to operate correctly in presence of faults. Use mechanism to avoid errors being propagated. Can implement automatic recovery from errors.

5.2   Different proposals

Some previous most general software models have been included at the beginning in order to compare them with the ones focused on cloud systems. From the literature most of the presented models are based in traditional systems dependability models, including traditional information systems dependability and reliability models. As said some of these traditional dependability models (M. Xie 2004) are not always valid for cloud computing, mainly because of the complexity of cloud systems.

5.2.1   Traditional software reliability models

These are standard models for software reliability. These models are mainly based on proposed distributions for reliability of systems. Most of these systems are based on other more complex systems. There have been different assessments by different authors like Goel (Goel 1985) about these types of models and their approach to software development and reliability of systems.

There are as well some issues with using these models for critical or very complex systems and specially systems that rely on cloud services. One issue is that some of these models assume that new faults are not introduced during the fault removal process, and this is not always true as systems can change when the removal of the fault is done, it is very difficult to ensure that new faults are introduced when the system is corrected. Another assumption of these models is that faults appear equally during the operation of a system, and this is not always the case as some parts can be executed more than others depending of external factors. They assume as well that testing is representative of the operational use, but this is not always true, as not always the test samples are relevant to the operational use, as a different user can execute different parts of the system. As well all these models require previous failure data made available, that is not always the case if part of the systems are completely new or the data is not provided by the vendor. Due to these assumptions and problems this type of models and frameworks are not suitable when using with cloud services.

5.2.1.1   Time between failures models

Jelinski and Moranda (Z. J. Moranda 1972) defined one of the most used models for assessing software reliability based on the time failures, assuming that there are N software faults at the start of the testing, where each is independent of others and is similarly likely to cause a failure. The software failure rate at any time is proportional to the current fault content of the program. There are variations like the proposed by Moranda (P. B. Moranda 1975) where faults are not removed until there is a fatal occurrence; at that point the group of faults is removed. Schick and Wolverson (Wolverton 1973) propose a model based on the assumptions of the Jelinski and Moranda model, but in this case the hazard function is assumed to be proportional to the current fault content of the program as well as to the time elapsed since the last failure. The Goel and Okumon (Goel, Amrit L.; Okumoto, Kazu 1979) Imperfect debugging model is an extension of the Jelinski and Moranda one but overcoming the limitation that others have when assuming that the faults are removed with certainty when detected, treating the faults in the system as a Markov process model where the transition probabilities are governed by the probability of imperfect debugging.

As with the previous type of models, these assume as well that testing is representative of the operational use, and as well require previous failure data made available, which is not always the case if part of the systems is completely new or the vendor does not provide the data. Due to these assumptions and problems this type of models and frameworks are not suitable when using with cloud services.

5.2.1.2   Fault count models

These try to model the number of failures detected in a given testing interval, so when faults are removed from the system the number of failures per unit time will decrease. Most of them are based on a Poisson distribution. Shooman

(Shooman 1972) propose one of the first models from this type. Musa (Musa 1971) proposed a similar one but this time based on execution time. Goel and Okumoto (Okumoto 1978) proposed a time dependent failure rate of the Poisson process and developed the details of the model.

These models as well cannot be used properly for cloud computing because they assume that testing is representative of the operational use, and as well require previous failure data made available, that is not always the case if part of the systems is completely new or the data is not provided by the vendor.

5.2.1.3   Input domain and Fault injection based models

Both types of models are based on testing of the system. In input domain models, a set of test cases is generated from an input distribution. In Nelson (Nelson 1978) model the reliability of the software is measured by running the software for a sample of n randomly chosen inputs from the input domain based on a probability distribution obtaining a reliability estimate of the software based on the number of inputs that resulted in execution failures. Ramamoorthy and Bastani presented a model (Bastani 1982) for critical real-time software, providing an estimate of the conditional probability that the software is correct for a specific set of inputs.

In fault injection models, a known number of faults are injected (seeded) in the program, after testing, the number of injected and native faults is counted. Using combination and maximum likelihood estimation, the number of native faults and reliability of the software can be estimated. Mills proposed the Hypergeometric model (Mills. 1972). The model requires that a number of known faults be randomly injected in the system to be tested during some time. The number of injected and native faults discovered during the test by the hypergeometric distribution can estimate the number of native faults.

This is the last of the traditional type of reliability and dependability models, and present similar assumptions that make them not suitable for cloud computing because they assume that testing is representative of the operational use, and as well require previous failure data made available, that is not always the case if part of the systems is completely new or the data is not provided by the vendor.

5.2.2   Dai et al. Holistic Cloud reliability model

This cloud model is taking into account a holistic view of the cloud service. Dai et al. (Yuan-Shun Dai 2010). They classify the possible failures in two categories, depending on when the failures can occur before or after the assignation to the resource. The request stage failures that includes overflow and timeouts and the execution stage failures that includes resources missing, software and hardware failures. The model covers two stages, the request stage and the execution stage. For the request stage they follow a Markov model. For the execution stage they propose a new graph model and a new algorithm based on graph theory and Bayesian theorem. The graph model will permit to address all main different failures in a holistic way during the execution phase and the algorithm evaluate the overall cloud service reliability in the execution phase. It is necessary anyhow to have detailed information including working times about all elements, as well as a clear design and knowledge of all parts of the model. This is not always possible for customers.

5.2.3   Abbadi Operational Trust in clouds

Imad M. Abbadi (Abbadi 2011) proposes the assessment of operational trust for cloud services. Abbadi defines a set of properties that will define the trustiness of the cloud service. The properties are adaptability (reaction to infrastructure and application changes), resilience when components fail, scalability of the infrastructure, availability of the service and reliability. He defines functions in order to calculate the value for each property and an operational cloud provider trust is calculated. These values of each cloud provider can be used for assess them. The proposal can be used for assess properties like reliability without the need of having internal information of the cloud system. This model does not present a way on how to automatically react on this information, and as well there is no clear definition of how the information is collected and how different sources of information can be merged when values are coming from different vendors.

5.2.4   CloudSim

Calheiros et al. (Calheiros 2011) define a simulation approach to the evaluation of attributes like performance of Cloud services in a repeatable manner under varying system and user configurations. They proposed to use an extensible simulation toolkit that enables modelling and simulation of Cloud computing systems and application provisioning environments, that they call cloudSim. The proposed toolkit supports modelling and simulation of Cloud computing environments consisting of both single and inter-networked clouds (federation of clouds). This simulation tool permits evaluating the hypothesis (application benchmarking study) in a controlled environment where one can easily reproduce results. This approach is different from the one presented in this work where a real environment is used and data from other real environments are used.

Cloudsim takes a holistic approach, giving the possibility of taking into account different infrastructure and services in the model. However, it is mainly based in the resource provisioning modelling. IT can be used for low level and high level modelling, but it is not designed to be integrated to operate with operational environments and apply actions based on SLAs or predefined rules. It can be considered as fault pretension and fault removal as most of the work is done during the design phase.

5.2.5   Lin and Chang reliability for a cloud computing network Patent

Yi-Kuei Lin and Ping-Chen Chang have a patent (Chang 2012) for the estimation method for reliability evaluation of a cloud-computing network. It is focused in the network side of utilizing the cloud service and how to measure the reliability. It uses a model of the cloud-computing network, and includes for each edge (network connection or physical cable) a maintenance cost. Using vectors for different paths (at least two paths) taking into account the load capacity and the transmission time. According to different maintenance budgets and corresponding system reliability, the system supervisor could determine a reasonable maintenance budget to maintain a good level of quality and reliability of the cloud system. From the perspective of system design, the system supervisor could further conduct a sensitivity analysis to improve or investigate the most important part in a large cloud system based on system reliability.

This system is focused in the network side of a cloud system, not taking into account other parts of the system like software or hardware reliability or dependency on other cloud systems. It could be considered as a micro model because it permits the reliability of the network of a specific cloud system, but does not include the integration with different type of systems or cloud vendors. It can be used during the operational part of the system, once it has been deployed in production. The model is mainly getting the monitoring values from only one type of system. It does not define the use of web to specify the performance metrics associated with a service. In order to improve the dependability it uses fault prevention and fault forecasting.

5.2.6   Almahad et al. SLA Framework for cloud computing

Almahad et al. (Alhamad, Dillon and Chang 2010) define the use of dynamic SLA metrics for different groups of cloud users. They define SLA metrics for IaaS (e.g.

response time), PaaS (e.g. scalabiliy), SaaS (e.g. reliability) and Storage as a Service (e.g. system throughput). As well they define general SLA metrics that can be used for any type of cloud service (e.g. support service, security). In a second stage, they define how the negotiation of the SLA can be done. By direct negotiation or a trusted agent, this could add added value to the service by monitoring all or some of the SLA parameters.

This framework could be used in a holistic approach as it could be used to monitor and get metrics from different part of the system and the system as a whole. However the framework in more focused in a micro model than a macro approach, not defining a way of having different systems and putting together the information of these different systems.

5.2.7   Gustavsson and Sta SLA for Critical infrastructures

Gustavsson and Sta (Gustavsson and Stå hl 2010) introduce the concept of using cloud services for Critical Infrastructure, in particular for smart grid. They explain the issues of using very complex and dynamic systems, and the challenges of controlling them where used in Critical Infrastructures. They introduce the use of SLAs as mechanisms of high-level coordination between the different stakeholders and monitoring of regulatory policies. For the implementation they propose the use of SLA-Agents using the JACK industry standard, as well as the EXP-II implementation. The model is mainly focused in the smart grid, not having a holistic approach for Cloud systems.

5.2.8   Xu and Wang cooperative monitoring for Internet Data Centers

Other approaches are focused in the use of empiric data, mainly from monitoring, and sometimes use this data together with information from models. Xu and Wang (Wang 2008) define the cooperative monitoring for Internet Data Centers. Using an algorithm for locating monitor nodes for the purposes of load balancing and resilience. The algorithm is based on distributed hash tables for locating the monitor nodes, and analyzes its performance through simulations based on the dataset collected from a large Internet service provider. The benefits of this model are that the monitoring load is shared and that is more resilient that normal centralized monitoring approaches, but it is mainly focused in load balancing of monitoring, not in what to do with those values.

5.2.9   Park et al. monitoring service for fault tolerance in mobile cloud

Park et al. (JiSu Park 2011) use a Markov chain based monitoring service for fault tolerance in mobile cloud computing. The monitoring technique analyses and predicts resource states, doing the cloud system more resistant to the fault problem caused by the volatility of the mobile devices making a prediction of a future state. This technique is in part similar to the reliability problems presented in cloud environments. The technique models the patterns of operations performed in the past and predict the type of future operation states, thus providing data that can be used for fault tolerance, improving the reliability and performance of the system.

The model is focused for mobile devices in cloud services, because they are considered more instable, it does not have a holistic approach, and it is based in more detail (micro) level of these devices. It mainly is used for get information about the current system using monitoring of specific metrics, and using this to get information for improving the system.

5.2.10 Song Fu framework for autonomic anomaly detection in the cloud

Another approach is the one presented by Song Fu (Fu 2011) where a framework for autonomic anomaly detection in the cloud is defined. Information from different nodes is used to measure the relevance and redundancy among the large number of performance metrics available. The approach of reusing data from monitoring systems and predicting the impact in the future is similar to the one presented in the book. The framework selects the most relevant metrics and limits the amount of labelled data, for later identify anomalies in the cloud using a semi-supervised decision tree detection mechanism. The framework is focused in the selection of metrics and how to reduce the amount of data, but cannot be used for SLA measuring and automatic actions based on the result of the metrics.

5.2.11 Pietrantuono et al. Online monitoring of system Reliability

This monitoring approach (Pietrantuono, Russo and Trivedi 2010) gives an estimate of the actual reliability of the system in operation, and this is compared with the expected reliability. This approach combines the traditional reliability modelling approach with the dynamic monitoring and analysis when the system is in operation to periodically evaluate the system reliability trend. For the first part it uses a state-based model, a discrete time Markov chain model (DTMC) to represent the software architecture of the system to study. For the dynamic analysis they use the Daikon inferential engine. Once the system is operational, they calculate the runtime reliably and compare it with the expected reliability, and if it is lower, an alarm is triggered.

The monitoring approach is similar to the one proposed in this book. The model is more focus in architecture of a single system. Does not offer a holistic approach that could monitor different aspects of the system, and is focused mainly on the reliability of the components. It supports operational phase of the system, but the actions that the system can do is restricted to the triggered of alarms.

5.2.12   Undheim et al. cloud SLA availability model

The authors (Undheim, Chilwan and Heegaard 2011) define an overall availability model for a cloud system, defining the need for a better definition of the KPIs (Key performance indicators) used for availability and taking into account the network availability. It is focused on how the SLAs for Cloud datacentres and vendors are calculated and how can be improved. According to the authors, SLAs should be available on demand, being as well adjustable on demand. Two of the possible dimensions for differentiating cloud applications are the deployment of replicas in different physical locations and how different applications need different fault tolerance schemes

5.3   Conclusion of the Estate of the Art

As we can see from Table 1, none of the current models and frameworks presented solves the proposed problem. Some of them rely on previous data to be used for the model, other are focus in systems where the level of detail is high, but the level of abstraction is low; and others in the opposite, but not permitting to combine both, thus not solving the problem of evaluating the resilience and reliability of systems interacting with cloud services were not enough data of those services are known.

Models / evaluation	Holistic Approach	Micro Model	Macro Model	Operational phase usage	Action-based Feedback Auto	Multi-source monitoring	Automatic SLA	Comments
Time between failures models	N	Y	N	N	N	N	N	Traditional software model based on distribution
Fault count models	N	Y	N	N	N	N	N	Traditional software model based on distribution
Input domain models	N	Y	N	N	N	N	N	Traditional software model based on distribution
Fault injection models	Y	Y	Y	N	N	N	N	
Lin and Chang Patent	N	Y	N	Y	N	N	N	Focused on network access to cloud system
Dai et al. Holistic Cloud reliability model	Y	Y	N	Y	N	N	N	Holistic approach but needed detailed information of all parts
Abbadi Operational Trust in clouds	Y	N	Y	Y	N	N	Y	Not defined how to monitor services, not feedback actions
Simulation: CloudSim	Y	Y	Y	N	N	N	N	Mainly valid in the design phase, to simulate its behaviour in cloud.
Almahad et al. SLA Framework for cloud	Y	Y	N	Y	Y	N	Y	Using SLAs in operational mode to control the system
Gustavsson SLA for Critical infrastructures	N	Y	N	Y	N	Y	Y	Focused on the smart grid, both the generation and distribution
Cooperative monitor Internet Data Centers	N	Y	N	Y	N	Y	N	Mainly dealing with the load balancing and resilience of monitor
Park et al. monitoring service fault tolerance	N	Y	N	Y	N	N	N	Used for monitoring mobile cloud services, not holistic approach
Song Fu framework for autonomic anomaly detection in the cloud	N	Y	N	Y	N	N	N	Good definition of the algorithm for detection of anomalies
Online monitoring of system Reliability	N	Y	N	Y	Y	N	N	Operational and static modelling. Actions focused on triggers.
Undheim et al. cloud SLA availability model	N	Y	N	Y	N	N	N	Focused on SLAs for availability. Does not define a monitoring strategy
MMRF (Our model)	Y	Y	Y	Y	Y	Y	Y	

Table 8. Models and Frameworks for system reliability evaluation state of the art

As explained in the definition of the problem, the existing reliability assessment models and frameworks can be useful during the design phase of a system with cloud computer. Early approaches using statistical models likes the ones based on hardware, or the ones based on component based systems that get the reliability of each component does not adapt well to the new architecture models like cloud computing. Previous models do not consider the influence of the system usage and the execution environment.

As more cloud automation and dynamic selection of cloud services are becoming common, it makes sense to move to models that can be adapted in the operational phase. This will permit to the systems that use the cloud vendors to be more dynamic. These models could make use of runtime monitoring and prediction, taking into consideration both quantitative and qualitative information of the cloud services. For this reason there is the need of a new framework that could be used for the study and analysis of the resilience, reliability and dependability of cloud services, and that could be used for different cloud vendors.

5.3.1   Macro-Micro Resilience Framework (MMRF): Proposed Framework

The MMRF is the framework that will be presented in this book. The framework is based on the concepts of macro and micro dependability that are defined later. It defines entities that can be providers, consumers, or monitoring entities, and an entity can have more than one role. Each role has a few characteristics that will define how this role operates and the reliability/dependability of that entity for that role. The attributes should be simple to describe and to allocate a measure that could be validated by the monitoring roles of the entities. These monitoring roles can be allocated to an external entity that corroborates the previous allocation by the entity, in a similar way to certification authorities.

The framework has a holistic approach, studying the system as a whole and taking into account as many parts of the system as required. This framework can be used for Micro Models (low level of abstraction/ detail level is high), thus permitting the use of the framework for more detailed and specific scenarios. As well can be used for Macro Models (abstraction is high/ detail level low), and combines both micro and macro models and be able to use them together to get better understanding of the systems, and be able to use more detailed data when there is the possibility.

The framework can be used in the operational phase of the system, permitting to enhance the framework once the system is operational. The framework can use feedback from how is working in real time to execute different actions automatically, providing the framework of a way to act directly into the system based on the information from the current subsystems, giving the possibility of improve the resilience of the system once it is in operation. As well the framework supports multiple-source monitoring; getting information from different sources, some of them validated by authorities to obtain monitoring values that can be used for the calculation of the resilience and reliability values. It uses automatic SLA system to obtain and check the SLA values to confirm that are within the agreement and if not take automatic actions. Regarding the dependability mean, it is Fault prevention, fault forecasting and fault removal.

"The cheapest, fastest, and most reliable components
of a computer system are those that aren't there."

[G. Bell]

6 Proposed Macro-Micro Resilience Framework (MMRF)

6.1   Introduction

The lack of control over all the complete supply chain has been the base for the proposed model, where the dependencies between different parts of the cloud services are defined. As organizations move more services to the cloud, the impact in their internal complexity and in the reliability of the systems they are offering to the organization itself and their clients will increase. Not always this added complexity and associated risks to their reliability are seen.

The current fault models for studying dependability and fault analysis are not valid anymore for all cases. In part due to the complexity of the systems, it is not easy to get all the information about all components of the model and use one of the old models to find if a system will work properly, so system simulation or fault injections are other directions in dependability and fault analysis.

This chapter defines the proposed framework. The first section describes the Macro and Micro dependability and the differences when getting dependability information between traditional systems that are well known and implemented in-house and the ones that use cloud services. The next section describes the framework and the different phases, with their inputs and outputs. Following is the explanation of the different types of organization and the entities used in the framework. The next section explains how these entities interact, with the possible links used by the framework. Once the entities and interactions are explained, some examples of possible rules used for calculation of different attributes like availability or dependability for both macro and micro scenarios are described. The two last topics describe the metrics used and the types of attributes that could be used to measure these metrics.

6.2   Macro and Micro Dependability

When two or more CI systems are interacting, the risks of one can propagate to the rest, distributing the risks. The term micro-dependability is used by us here to define this concept; micro-dependability is defined in the context of Computer Systems as the relations of the Computer systems inside organizations that could effect on the reliance of the services that these deliver. However, most of these systems could be part of a bigger system, that can be a Critical Infrastructure, in some cases these boundaries and connections are not clear, and only when real problems appear is when the connection of these systems as part of the critical systems are seen, but sometimes is too late to avoid the disaster. So moving to cloud systems, in a more subtle way, could impact the complexity and the reliability of these Critical systems, even when initially the change was better for the organization due to other reasons like cost reduction.

The other term that has been introduced is Macro-dependability, and is defined in this book to refer to how the reliability of a system (including Critical Systems) could be affected when changes are done in some parts of other Systems. In the case of macro-dependability the relations are not inside but within systems of other organizations or bigger systems, and how these could influence the reliance of the services that these deliver. The main problem with both concepts, but specially the second, is that this could be happening now for companies managing critical systems, including Critical Infrastructure services and they will not know the risks until probably is too late, as Egan described for the rafted networks (Egan 2007).

Similar terms to the ones used in economy are used by us because the way it works for economy for both micro and macro economy, when you do changes in something that could affect the economy of the organization, usually these changes affect initially to the organization, but when this changes are done by more or in specific (or critical) areas could even affect to bigger systems and even the society or the economy of bigger areas (region, country, world).

6.3   MMRF: Macro & Micro Resilience Framework

The existing frameworks are not always relevant when dealing with the different types of systems. The purpose is to apply different types of rules and interactions for both types. Micro-dependability usually operates inside the organization and the scope is well defined. It could use traditional models and analysis methods (SysML ,FTA,RBD,PHA) (Linhares, et al. 2007). Macro-dependability instead is applied when the system is part of a bigger system and the details are unknown. In this case the use of traditional methods is not always possible, so new methods and rules to define cloud interactions, based for example on provider's actual measure through monitoring (WSLA) of specific operational attributes of the service offered. This information could be produced and provided by independent parties that could validate it.

The proposed framework presents both concepts of macro and micro dependability and try to put them together in order to not only consider what it is known and studied using traditional models, but the part that we do not normally see and it is operated by external parties such as cloud service providers.

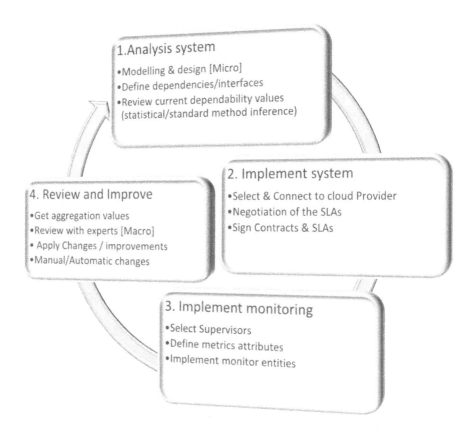

Figure 14 - Phases of the MMRF Framework

The proposed framework is based in a Deming (Deming 1986) do-plan-check/study-act cycle; it is represented in Figure 14 - Phases of the MMRF Framework. The framework can be used for reviewing the dependability measures (availability, reliability, etc..) for a Macro-Micro critical system (from now on called the system) using internal services plus cloud services from one or more providers. The MM system will have interfaces or be implemented in cloud services. The studied critical system has micro and macro dependability interactions. Micro with the internal organization and as part of other critical process or systems and macro because it uses external cloud services where only the main interfaces are known.

The cycle is formed by four iterative different phases, for each of them their inputs and outputs are presented:

- 1. System analysis: In this phase we will review the system to be implemented, and what are the main entities of the system. If the system were a new one, there would be a design and development process as part of this phase. We should define the dependencies of the system as well as review current dependability (reliability/availability/resilience) values for the system. At this stage we will focus more in the internal part of the system, up to the interfaces with the cloud providers. Once this stage is finished we will have a representation of the system (e.g.SysUML) indicating what parts of the system will be implemented internally and what will use cloud services. At this stage we will have the definition of the attributes that we will use to measure the system, and information of these attributes for the internal parts of the systems (micro-dependability) and estimation for the external part in cloud vendors.
    - o Inputs:
        - Previous diagrams of the system (if exists)
        - Information about cloud vendors (if exists)
    - o Outputs:
        - Diagram of the system SysUML with cloud interaction (interfaces)
        - List of producers and consumers entities that will be used
            - Cloud providers that will be used
        - List of dependability expected values for each Service that will be used

- 2. System implementation: We will implement the proposed system, and connect to the cloud vendors that we have chosen in the previous phase. Part of this phase will imply the signature of contracts and definition and agreement of the SLAs with the external cloud vendors for the Macro-dependability. Organizations must have a clear policy regarding the control of assets for critical items. This should include the proper identification and documentation of these assets, together with the ownership and the impact on the critical items. This will permit to define clearly responsibilities and distinction of the responsibilities during the operational phase.

- o Inputs:
  - Diagram of the system with cloud interfaces
  - Cloud providers that will be used
  - List of dependability values for each Service that will be used
- o Outputs:
  - List of entities with the detailed information of the interfaces
  - SLAs expected values for the metrics
  - Cloud providers with SLAs / WSLAs agreements of the cloud provider

- 3. Monitoring Implementation: Until this phase, the design and implementation of the system will not differ too much of a traditional way of doing it, using traditional methods for analysing the system. In this phase we will define and select the supervisor and monitoring entities that will check the selected metrics for the different cloud vendors. It is here when the different rules for the micro and macro domains as well as the aggregation of monitoring values will be defined.
  - o Inputs:
    - Diagram of the system SysUML with cloud interaction (interfaces)
    - List of cloud providers chosen
    - List of SLAs and dependability expected values
  - o Outputs:
    - List of chosen Supervisors and monitoring entities
    - Definitive list of metrics attributes to monitor

- 4. Monitoring reviewing: Once the monitoring values are implemented and working properly we will review if the aggregation is working properly and the values are according to what is expected. Experts of the domains can review these values in order to confirm that are according to what is expected from the system. There is the possibility of apply automatic changes to the system based on the values of the monitoring entities, like for example change a cloud provider for a specific interface if the values are not in the expected range.

- o Inputs:
  - Diagram of the system SysUML with cloud interaction (interfaces)
  - List of cloud providers chosen
  - List of SLAs and dependability expected values
  - List of chosen Supervisors and monitoring entities
  - Definitive list of metrics attributes to monitor
- o Outputs:
  - Changes proposed to the system/implementation
  - Changes proposed to the list of metrics attributes to monitor
  - Updated list of expected values

The framework is implemented as a cycle. Once the last phase has been finished and there is enough information to take decisions, these will be implemented together in a new cycle as other phase one. The subsequent cycles will usually be more focused on the macro-dependability parts and especially in the interaction with the cloud services. Revision and changes in the micro-dependability, even if are less common, could happen in cases such as replacing some of the services provided internally for services provided by external cloud providers.   Figure 15 - Inputs and outputs of each phase of the Framework shows the main inputs and outputs for each phase of the system.

A very important part of the framework is the definition of a standard network of monitoring authorities that could provide monitoring data about the services exposed by cloud vendors and could independently validate the results for each service. It could be implemented in a similar way the certification authority's network for PKI certificates (Vacca 2004). Currently there are some providers, normally monitoring providers that offer something similar, but this are still very immature and there is still a lack of standards that could be used by all vendors and customers in order to interchange this monitoring information about the operation status of these services. Some initiatives like WSLA (P. Patel 2009) have been created to solve this issue. These entities could monitor and validate not only standard values like availability or performance, but other values like reliability or resilience using specific mechanisms with the cloud provider without making this information public. Specific load tests, component failure simulation and security attacks could be done in a controlled environment by these monitoring entities. The information will be published and used automatically (WSLA) by customers in order to take decisions when these values change according to pre-defined rules.

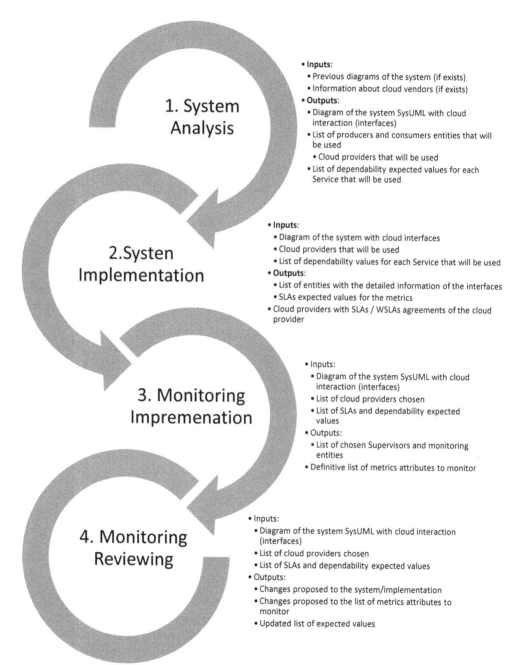

1. System Analysis

- Inputs:
  - Previous diagrams of the system (if exists)
  - Information about cloud vendors (if exists)
- Outputs:
  - Diagram of the system SysUML with cloud interaction (interfaces)
  - List of producers and consumers entities that will be used
    - Cloud providers that will be used
  - List of dependability expected values for each Service that will be used

2.Systen Implementation

- Inputs:
  - Diagram of the system with cloud interfaces
  - Cloud providers that will be used
  - List of dependability values for each Service that will be used
- Outputs:
  - List of entities with the detailed information of the interfaces
  - SLAs expected values for the metrics
  - Cloud providers with SLAs / WSLAs agreements of the cloud provider

3. Monitoring Impremenation

- Inputs:
  - Diagram of the system SysUML with cloud interaction (interfaces)
  - List of cloud providers chosen
  - List of SLAs and dependability expected values
- Outputs:
  - List of chosen Supervisors and monitoring entities
  - Definitive list of metrics attributes to monitor

4. Monitoring Reviewing

- Inputs:
  - Diagram of the system SysUML with cloud interaction (interfaces)
  - List of cloud providers chosen
  - List of SLAs and dependability expected values
- Outputs:
  - Changes proposed to the system/implementation
  - Changes proposed to the list of metrics attributes to monitor
  - Updated list of expected values

Figure 15 - Inputs and outputs of each phase of the Framework

Table 9 could be used by an automated process in order to decide what is the vendor that meets the minimum expected attributes with the minimum costs.

Cloud Provider	Cost (€)	Availability (%)			Response Time (ms.)			Time to Recover (in case incident) (min)		
		Target	Initial	Cycle1	Target	Initial	Cycle1	Target	Initial	Cycle1
Vendor1	900	99.99	99.999	99.997	0.9	0.998	0.954	2	14	10
Vendor2	800		99.998	99.999		0.894	0.913		1	4
Vendor3	700		99.995	99.996		0.918	0.984		67	34

Table 9 Example of cloud vendors providing the same service with attributes measured

The framework is based in an online and shared model provided by independent parties (mainly monitoring authorities) that can be used by different organizations to get information about the dependability, availability, reliability, resilience and other characteristics of the cloud services. The idea is to use the standard models more focused on the design and construction phase for getting the micro-dependability part and use a different approach for the macro-dependability, based on testing and operational phases.

6.4   Organization and Entities

Our model defines the relations of the entities inside organizations with other providers (like cloud services). A very simple diagram system is used for represent the different organizations and entities, an example is provided in fig.4.

The main organization types are:

- Providers (e.g. Amazon): We use this term usually for the organizations that provide services. Normally will be cloud providers, but these can be other type or organization. There could be providers that aggregate different providers. This is the case of providers that join together to offer specific services that one alone could not offer. There can be as well providers that use other services from different providers.

- Customers (e.g. pharmaceutical company): organization that will normally consume the services offered by the providers. In some cases the customers can produce services that are used by other organizations. Customers as well connect to the supervisors to get information about the services that will be used.

- Supervisors (e.g. Certification Authority): organizations that will mainly monitor producers and aggregate data about the different services offered by the providers. These organizations will normally charge for their services.

Each organization can have different type of entities. Entities can be producers, consumers, or monitoring entities and an organization can have more than one role. The supervisors could have a similar role to the one that now Certification Authorities have. This is one of the main differences with the current systems used for monitoring, where the values are provided by internal monitoring systems or external companies, but cannot be properly verified. Normally automatic actions like change the cloud provider cannot based on automatic actions due to the changes in these metrics.

The main entity types are:

- Producer: entity that offers services can be infrastructure services like in the case of IaaS or software services in the case of SaaS or PaaS. In both cases there should have defined the properties or attributes that offer. As an example for a virtual server the number of virtual CPUs, or the memory allocated. For software usually indicates the interfaces and behaviour. Services can be aggregated/nested to form new services.

- Consumer: request and use services from producers. Most of the organizations (does not matter if they are customer or providers) will have consumer entities, as it will use services from other producers.

- Monitoring entity: the entity that is responsible of monitoring a service. Normally has a definition of the different services to monitor and the different metrics to use for each service.

An entity will match with a service that can be consumed or will be used. Each role has a few attributes or characteristics that will define how this role operates and the reliability/dependability of that entity for that role. The attributes should be simple to describe and to allocate a measure that could be validated by the monitoring roles of the entities. These monitoring roles can be allocated to an external entity that corroborates the previous allocation by the entity.

An initial diagram can be created during the first phase that will include all the different organizations, entities, services and attributes to be monitored. This will include the internal organization and the external organizations such as cloud vendors. For each organization all the main entities will be included, and for each entity all the attributes that will or could be monitored will be measured. The last part is to include the interactions, both the dependency interactions and the monitoring ones. This diagram will be used in the following phases to review the MM System and improve it.

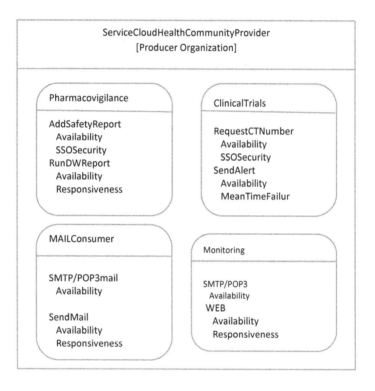

An example organization is shown in Figure 16 Example of an entity for a cloud community provider with producers, consumers and monitor services. The organization is a community provider that has been created between different governmental organizations for provide monitoring and authorization services for pharmacovigilance and critical trials. In this fictitious example two services provided by this organization (cloud provider) have been created. In the entity are two main services that produce services that other organizations can use. For example, for the service pharmacovigilance there are two main subservices,

AddSafetyReport used for adding new safety reports for an adverse reaction of a drug. In this example, there are a few attributes that are interesting from the reliability and dependability point of view, as well as for the monitoring of that service. Other entities (organizations) or the same one can consume those services. In this example the entity has a consumer service that is used for managing the email with other providers (like a company that provides messaging services).

The use of other services of different providers is very common, and is using these other services where the interdependencies are more difficult to control. The use is more normal in a cloud model, where services are specific and are becoming more specialized. Email is a good example; currently there are companies like Messagelabs that provide antivirus, antispam scanning or encryption of email. The consumer organization uses the services, and only is interested in a few metrics like availability, responsiveness and effectiveness, but not in parameters like the type of infrastructure that this producer organization is using to support the services, or where the physical service is located.

The third type of service for an entity is the monitoring service; in this case there is a small monitoring service for the web interfaces and for email. In this example these two could be used for internal (web) or external (email) services, and for each monitoring service there are some attributes that are monitored. This permits to have information that can be used and shared with other monitoring services from other organizations in order to get information about the reliability of those services offered by the provider. This is more useful if the monitoring organization is an external independent one.

6.5   Macro and Micro Dependability interactions

Other information that is not shown in the previous figure is the relation between the entities. Usually the consumers will connect to producers to use the services. This information in shown in the diagrams using links between consumers and producers, and from the point of view of reliability and dependability it is the most important. In the previous example only one entity is shown, with no interactions between each entity services. In reality, there are interactions, as well as monitoring of these services. These interactions and the dependencies between different systems of the organization define micro-dependability for that organization. These are rules that are clearly defined and can be obtained using the traditional methods for dependability calculation. And once that these interactions are recorded, it will be simple to track dependencies of one service with other, as well as to monitor them.

These diagrams are normally created during phase one, but will be refined in the following phases. The diagrams can be nested, that implies that the values are aggregated. The interactions between different systems of the organizations define dependability, with information from monitoring. The diagrams and the interaction between the entities on the diagrams help to understand better the different dependencies with external systems. These diagrams and interactions can be reused by different consumers, and can be offered by the supervisors as part of their services. One of the issues is the problem of representing the information about the dependencies of a cloud provider, mainly because usually the providers do not disclose this information as they consider this part of their know-how. One advantage is that when disclosed, the supervisors can have this information, keep it, validate it and updated. In this way they can offer this to consumers to verify the different values of the attributes during the first two phases before choosing the provider for the cloud services. This could be extremely useful for critical services.

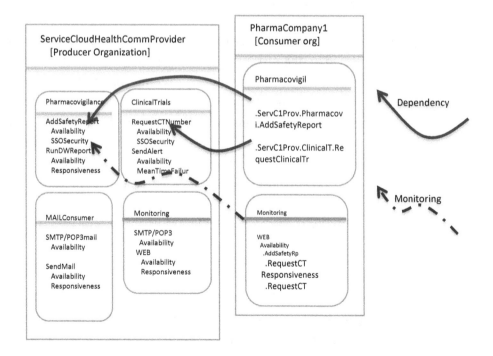

Figure 17 Example of interactions between one cloud producer organization and a cloud consumer

Continuing with the example of the cloud Community provider for Pharmacovigilance and clinical trials applications, in Figure 17 Example of interactions between one cloud producer organization and a cloud consumer; there is a consumer of the services as well. In this case the consumer can be an external organization that is acting as a consumer of both services of the cloud community provider. In this example, it is a pharmaceutical company that needs to send Safetyreports and request Clinical Trial approvals. There are two types of interaction or connections between the entities, the dotted line that is used for monitoring of services and should be indicated the interval for monitor, and the continuous lines that are used for expressing the real use of services from a consumer to a provider. It can be with more detail and other step can be explained in the link that will be the role of the consumer of the Service cloud community provider of services of an external cloud organization EmailServices that provides secure email services with antispam, virus free and extra mail services that the community provider needs to use. These services are consumed from other cloud organization because secure email services are not the core business of the Pharmacovigilance cloud community provider that is specialized on pharmacovigilance services only.

Now, in the diagrams we can see the links of the complete supply chain for these services that are provided, the attributes that are interested from the reliability point of view and the values of the monitoring from our point of view but from other providers of each of these attributes. This information can help to improve the risk assessment for the complete supply chain for that service. These connections/interactions between entities are mainly logical, and according to other interdependencies models [Rimaldi, 2004] will be "Logical Interdependencies", but others like geographic or physical could be added to the model.

6.6   Agents Implementation in the Framework

As explained in the previous sections, the framework used the different phases to get information about both micro and macro domains. In order to do that there are agents that are distributed over the different entities. These agents are defined for the supervisor, customer and providers and the main modules are:

- Definition: Responsible of maintain on the definition of the services, attributes and metrics, and aggregation rules both macro and micro and the security information for each metric. This information is defined typically defined by XML schemas created by Supervisor organization in collaboration with Providers. These can be downloaded to the rest of Agents in Customers and Providers to maintain a common metric and rule base. At Supervisor level the aggregation rules are mainly macro and at Customers level the aggregation extra aggregation rules will be defined to aggregate macro and micro rules.

- Measurement: This module is responsible of executing the measurement of the metrics defined by the definition module. It will get the values for the metrics defined for each service and monitor them according to the designated time intervals. Providers have specific measurements that will be only used by them (such as clusterNetworkTroughput) for calculation of aggregation values (micro rules) and where only these aggregated values are exposed to the supervisors and customers.

- Aggregation: Module responsible of the aggregation of the metrics based on the rules (macro and micro). Applies the aggregation of the values based on the time intervals defined on the metrics and with the rule defined on the aggregated metric for that service.

- Reporting: This module shows information for each Provider/service/attribute/metric. It permits to group the information and represent it in different ways to take decisions during the phase 4 of the framework. An example would be the aggregate metric AverageResponsiveness of service GetSafetyReports provided by two Providers. We could get a report by the two vendors with the values of the last month of the metric together with the values of the cost by month of the service to help to decide what service to choose in the next cycle.

The agent's modules expose web services using a Service Oriented Architecture that can be used over http. Locally stores the information using xml on files or a relational database to store the information about attributes and metrics definitions, rules, and SLA aggregations.

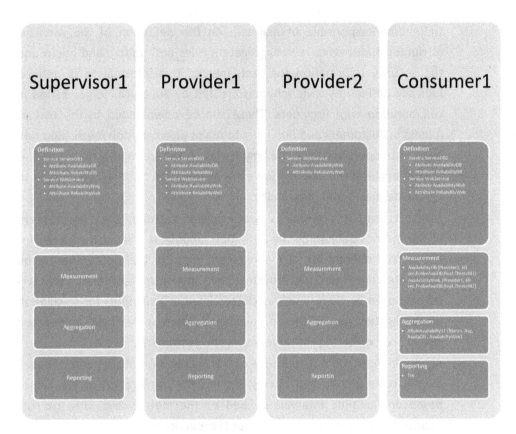

6.7   Macro & Micro Dependability Rules

During phase one, and as part of the definition of the services there should be included the attributes and rules that will be applied for these attributes. When calculating the dependability and its different characteristics like resilience, reliability and availability we will need to take into account type of domains and rules that will govern those domains. The micro dependability will be used as explained before for systems that are known and where traditional models can be applied. But when working with part of the systems where we do not have the full information about how it works or how it behaves in specific situations, like for example a cloud vendor we should use what we defined as macro dependability rules and values needs to be calculated in a different way.

As part of the phase one for each entity, when these are defined, there should be included the definition of the Services that the entity will provide. The definition of the Service will be done differently depending of the type of domain:

- For macro domains (defined by external organizations):

- Service and attributes: by Provider (of the producer entity)

- Metrics and values: by Supervisors (Monitoring) based on Attributes defined in Producer entity by the provider.

- For micro domains (defined by the customer, internal organization):

  - Service, attributes, metrics and values defined by producer entity

Other important aspect is when different attributes need to be aggregated. An example will be if for example we are calculating the reliability of a cloud service that is composed of different other services with different reliability values. In order to calculate the definitive value it will be needed to aggregate the different ones. Regarding how is done the aggregation of monitored values from different sources:

- For macro domains: Done by Supervisor (monitoring entity), depending on metric and based on a weighted average. The supervisor entity will allocate different weights and do the aggregation.

- For micro domains: not always needed, only internal. If needed, the customer will aggregate them.

Other important part of the process is the publication of the results of SLA achievements:

- In macro domains: this is done by Supervisors (Monitoring entities). Web dashboards could be used with results for each provider SLA achievement and optionally cost.

- For micro domains: this is optional, as normally these will not be published.

Adding new consumers will be done in the following way:

- Macro:

  - Customer should adjust monitoring metrics or get monitoring entity from monitoring supervisor (cost)

  - Assign weighing for new customer/consumers in monitoring entity

- Micro: Adjust current internal metrics to be in line with macro metrics, like values calculated with other techniques (RBD, FTA)

6.8   Attribute Metrics

It is important to define correctly the metrics that will be used in order to measure the attributes. These could be used as well for create the SLAs that will be agreed with the provider and in order to monitor if these SLAs are met. In this work the metrics are focused on the dependability, resilience and reliability, but others that could affect directly or indirectly should be added in a real scenario (cost, legal, security...). Some of the possible metrics that could be used are listed inFigure 18 Possible metrics that can be used for the attributes.

A few examples of the possible attributes for dependability are:

- Service Availability (Macro/Micro)
    - Mean time between failures
    - Incident rate
- Adaptability
    - Mean time to discover an incident (MTTD)
    - Mean time to invoke an action to remedy the incident (MTTI)
    - Mean time to recover an incident (MTTR)
    - Tolerance to attack
- Scalability (horizontal and vertical)
    - Mean time to procure resources
    - Mean time to deploy (MTTDp)
    - Mean time to scale up (MTSU)
    - Mean time to scale down (MTSD)

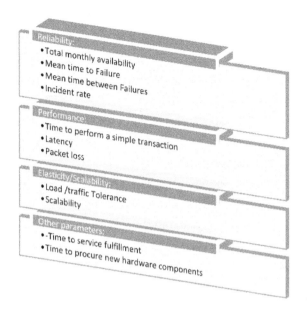

Figure 18 Possible metrics that can be used for the attributes

This information could be expressed using WSLA language defined by Keller (Keller 2002) and Patel (Patel 2009). Basically this will provide a mechanism to represent what will be monitored and control that is according to specific values that we have been agreed. Figure 19 shows an example of the definition of the metric by Monitoring Entity SOSMonitoring1: How many Values (in %) of a Utilization Time Series are over a Thresold of 90%:

```
<Metric name=OverloadPct" type="float" unit="Percentage">
    <DefinedMonitorEntity>SOSMonitoring1</DefinedMonitorEntity>
    <Source>Ymeasurement</Source>
    <Function xsi:type="PctGTThresold" resultType="float">
        <Schedule>BusinessDay</Schedule>
        <Metric>UtilizationTimeSeries</Metric>
        <Value>
                <LongScalar>0.9</LongScalar>
        </Value>
    </Function>
</Metric>
```

Figure 19 Example of WSLA definition of a monitoring entity SOSMonitoring1

The WSLA language is based on XML and could be extended to incorporate other functionality like rules for actions based on the expected values of the metrics and what can be done if these are not met.

6.9   Qualitative values for Reliability

For the aggregation of the services metrics there should be a clear definition of the attributes and metrics that will be used, and how these will be aggregated. As an example of a reliability attribute, in order to get quantitative values for the metrics of services attributes on the model we can use the reliability networks defined by Dhillon (Dhillon 2003) depending of the type of service that is offered (series, parallel, series-parallel, parallel-series and standby systems). In the example the services that the consumer Pharmaceutical companies use from the "Service Cloud Health Community Provider" Producer are at the same time using the mail services of other producer providing email with scan services, and only these, if this fails there is not a parallel Producer, in this case I use the series network, where the reliability is expressed as $R = R1\,R2\,R3...Rn$. So if the reliability of SendAlert is 0.95 and the SendEmail from the other provider is as well 0.95, the reliability of that function will be 0.8145. This will normally calculated by the supervisor if the provider provides the proper information and this could be validated.

Other models that could be applied are:

- Parallel in case of different services used in parallel so the Service will only fail when all the producers fail. R = 1 – (1-R1)(1-R2)(1-R3)...(1-Rn)

- Series-parallel, where the service is using n active sub-services (usually from that organization) in parallel.

- Parallel-series, in this case the service is using n other sub-services in parallel.

- Standby systems, where normally the service is using only one service, but there is a backup that is used if the main one fails.

 These should be applied first for the services of the organization (micro) and later once the values are calculated for the micro, use these for include other organizations (macro).

6.10   Conclusion of the proposed framework

In previous sections it has been explained that as organizations are moving services to the cloud the impact in their internal complexity and in the reliability of the systems they are offering to the organization itself and their clients will increase. Not always this added complexity and associated risks to their reliability are seen.

The current fault models for studying dependability and fault analysis are not valid anymore for all cases, in part due to the complexity of the systems, it is not easy to get all the information about all components of the model and use one of the old models to find if a system will work properly, so system simulation or fault injections are other directions in dependably and fault analysis.

As a possible solution to this problem a framework is presented. The framework is based in the concepts of two different types of domains. One called micro-dependability that is used to define the boundaries of the system that are known and could be studied by the organization itself using the standard existing methodologies. The second is the macro-dependability and is used to explain the domain that is not known normally because it is not managed by us, but by an external cloud vendor and it is offered as external cloud services. The risk created in the macro-dependability domain could be inherit now by companies managing critical systems, including Critical Infrastructure services and they will not know the risks until probably is too late, as Egan described for the rafted networks (Egan 2007).

The proposed framework is based in a Deming do-plan-check/study-act cycle. The framework can be used for reviewing the dependability measures (availability, reliability, etc..) for a critical system using a combination of a Macro and Micro dependability domains. The MM system will have interfaces or be implemented in cloud services. The studied critical system has micro and macro dependability interactions. Micro with the internal organization and as part of other critical process or systems and macro because it uses external cloud services where only the main interfaces are known.

A very important part of the framework is the concept of the organizations, entities, the roles of each one, and the interactions. One of the most important organization types is the Authorities. It explains the creation of a standard network of monitoring authorities that could provide monitoring data about the services exposed by cloud vendors and could independently validate the results for each service. Currently there are some providers, normally monitoring providers that offer something similar, but this are still very immature and there is still a lack of standards that could be used by all vendors and customers in order to interchange this monitoring information about the operation status of these services. Some initiatives like WSLA (P. Patel 2009) have been created to solve this issue. These entities could monitor and validate not only standard values like availability or performance, but other values like reliability or resilience using specific mechanisms with the cloud provider without making this information public. Specific load tests, component failure simulation and security attacks could be done in a controlled environment by these monitoring entities. The information will be published and used automatically (WSLA) by customers in order to take decisions when these values change according to pre-defined rules.

The framework is implemented as a cycle, once the last phase has been finish and there is enough information to take decisions the decisions will be implemented together in a new phase one. The subsequent cycles will usually been more focused on the macro-dependability parts and especially in the interaction with the cloud services. Revision and changes in the micro-dependability, even if are less common, could happen in cases such as replacing some of the services provided internally for services provided by external cloud providers. The four phases are system analysis, system implementation, monitoring implementation and monitoring reviewing.

Having a concept of public model where data about different characteristics of the cloud services (dependability, security, availability, performance) could be validated with external authorities could simplify the use of these services by critical systems. Service Level Agreements still will be valid but will cover other characteristics that currently are not covered (resilience, time to recover, security) and could be validated automatically and actions could be executed (like change provider) based on predefined rules related to these attributes and costs.

The concept is not easy to implement, as this will imply a wide scale implementation of standards for monitoring and sharing data about systems with monitoring authorities. As well, it will imply to regulate the role of these Authorities, as currently there is not a common approach to share this data and provide it to customers that could be used in operational time. Approach like WSLA defined by Keller (Keller 2002) and Patel (Patel 2009) could help to standardise this. There is still a long path to have something similar. But it is possible the only one if the use of these cloud services should be extended into other services like critical services, and the use of information as other utility (water, gas, electricity) is definitively adopted broadly.

"All models are wrong; some models are useful."

[G. Box]

7 An example: choosing a cloud service model for a critical system

7.1 Introduction

The proposed framework describes how the dependability between different cloud based systems interacts and how to monitor that this is met. As an example of a possible implementation of a critical system relaying on cloud services, we present how part of the implemenation could work for a real case, in this case a pharmacovigilance system.

In the recent years cloud computing is becoming a reality for almost all the ICT departments of all organizations. It is normal to hear that cloud computing have too many advantages to not use it. But the truth is that for most of the ICT departments where critical applications are running this is not always clear, and most do not even consider moving critical systems, including health systems like the one we are proposing here to be moved to the cloud. Cloud computing is changing the way the organizations are using computing resources, and ICT is starting to be considered for many organizations a utility, like electricity or water. But with all the spectrum of possibilities and different models and architectures how is possible to choose a model that meets our requirements and is cheaper. This section presents an example of a critical health system, a pharmacovigilance system, and what the options for moving to the cloud that system and how these solutions can be evaluated and implemented. This process could be applied to other similar types of systems in order to get more information about what type of cloud model and architecture would be the best one.

This is divided in two parts, the first one, where different proposals for implementation of the pharmacovigilance system are studied, taking into account the main requirements of the system, including costs. This does not pretend to replace a proper risk assessment methodology similar like the one propose by ENISA (Hogben Nov 2009) but the purpose is to give more information about the process of choosing different cloud models for a typical critical system.   In the second part, a proposed implementation of the pharmacovigilance system is done using the previous model and using the values obtained in part one for some of the requirements, in this case reliability the model is applied in order to look for possible risks on the reliability if the system is migrated to one of the cloud models.

For the implementation of the model a pharmacovigilance system will be presented for implementation into a cloud environment, taking three different architectures (SaaS, PaaS and IaaS) and three different models (private, public and community). This is a god example because is a critical system and now there are cases of implementations provided as cloud services by providers. Even if the topic is based on real systems the model has been simplified and the information that is used does not correspond to current real systems, as well a simplification of these systems has been done in order to streamline and understand better the applicability of the framework.

The focus will be in the study of the reliability of the implementations, but due to the importance and the interrelation with reliability it is included in the study other aspects like security, legal issues and cost.

7.2   Service Description

This section describes the service that has been used as an example for the framework. The service will be a pharmacovigilance system that is used at international level by pharmaceutical companies and healthcare professionals. The system should be deployed in the cloud and a few alternatives will be studied, using different cloud models and architectures. I will focus the model in reliability, but other attributes of the system will be explored, especially the ones that can affect dependability.

The main functional requirements of the proposed system on the cloud will be:

- FR1: Supports multi-tenancy (country, legislation)
- FR2: Supporting both Human and Veterinary
- FR3: Reporting capabilities (including regulatory reports)
- Methods supported for signal detection
  - FR4: Data mining capabilities (for a limited number of scientific administrators): extract meaningful, organized information, in this case signals, from large complex databases and has been used to identify hidden patterns of associations or unexpected occurrence in spontaneous reporting system databases

- o FR5: Case Series: evaluation of a series of case reports usually using specific algorithms that are commonly known. Proportional distributions, reporting rates, observed-to-expected analyses, case-control analyses, and survival analysis. Not all will be used, but at least one for this model should be used, in the future there should be the possibility of incorporate more and give reports based on different models.
- FR6: Use the ICH E2B standard for data elements of safety reports
- FR7: Receive files from different options (mail, ftp, web) (AS1, AS2, AS3) and different sources (pharmaceutical companies, regulatory authorities, individuals and GPs)
  - o XML Files received will be validated using a template
  - o Acknowledge of accepted and rejected messages will be send
- FR8: Use of (Medical Dictionary of Regulatory activities) MedDRA Coding and ISO IDMP Standards
- FR9: Receive Clinical trials reports as well
- Optional functional requirements:
  - o FRO1: Possibility of retrofit information from searches (itself or search providers like Google trends)
  - o FRO2: Possibility of integration with current health online systems like Google Health
  - o FRO2: Include possibility of add business rules created by the scientific administrators for specific tenant.

The main non-functional requirements are:

- NFR1: Integration with other gateway software
- NFR2: Access to the system from any web device
- NFR3: Availability is more than 99.9%, and for the reliability we will try to minimize the mean time to failure.
- NFR4: Encryption of information and secure access with possibility of strong authentication.
- NFR5: Response time is less than 0.9 for the GetSafetyReport service.
- NFR6: Time to recover is less than 2 minutes.

Roles of the users:

- R1: Safety evaluators
- R2: Scientific Administrators for the tenancy (country, countries)
- R3: ICT Administrators for the tenancy
- R4: Pharmaceutical companies
- Individuals
    - R5: healthcare professionals
    - R6: general public

Main modules of the system are:

- **Reporting/Data mining module**. This module is used for reporting and data mining capabilities (for a limited number of scientific administrators): extract meaningful, organized information, in this case signals, from large complex databases and has been used to identify hidden patterns of associations or unexpected occurrence in spontaneous reporting system databases.

- **Rule Parses**: It crawls trough the new safety reports in order to find patterns. Usually is implemented as services or daemons that run at specific intervals and connect to the database to get the data and process it. Permits the evaluation of a series of case reports usually using specific algorithms that are commonly known. Proportional distributions, reporting rates, observed-to-expected analyses, case-control analyses, and survival analysis. Not all will be used, but at least one for this model should be used, in the future there should be the possibility of incorporate more and give reports based on different models.

- **Web access module.** To permit the access to the system using web browser. It permits to execute certain functionalities trough a web interface.

- **Gateway/messages receiving module**. This module will receive the safety reports. It will be used AS1 (email), AS2 (http/s), and AS3 (FTPs) protocols, and there are different companies that provides out of the shelf solutions for these modules. All of the ASx protocols can:
    1. Encrypt a file using a recipient's public SSL certificate and sign the file using the sender's private SSL certificate
    2. Specify the type and manner of MDN that the recipient should return
    3. Deliver the file to a partner

4. Decrypt a file using a recipient's private SSL certificate and confirm the signature of the sender using the sender's public SSL certificate
5. Create an MDN delivery receipt signed with the recipient's private SSL certificate and containing a cryptographic hash of the file contents in order to prove that the recipient got the unaltered file
6. Return the MDN to the sender
7. Verify the MDN (against the recipient's public SSL certificate and the cryptographic hash) to absolutely prove that the recipient got the file.

The main module that will be used for the testing of the framework will be the gateway/messages-receiving module. The proposal is to implement this module using an external provider company that could host this functionality as a cloud service.

7.3   Current Pharmacovigilance system implementations

Currently there are different approaches in the implementation of Pharmacovigilance systems. The main approaches are in house development of a solution like the one done by the European Medicines Agency, or use of vendor software, like Oracle Argus Safety (Oracle 2011) chosen by Japan. Figure 20 Oracle Argus Insight Interface shows an example of the user interface of the Oracle Argus solution. Hybrid solutions could be used and is the one that is proposed for the example where the systems can be part in executing in the customer organization and part in external cloud vendors.

There are products that offer different pharmacovigilance functionality and interoperate with the current message standards like ICH:E2B and usually integrates with different tools for data analysis and data mining. These solutions provide multi-tenancy so they can be offered to different organizations in cloud community implementations.

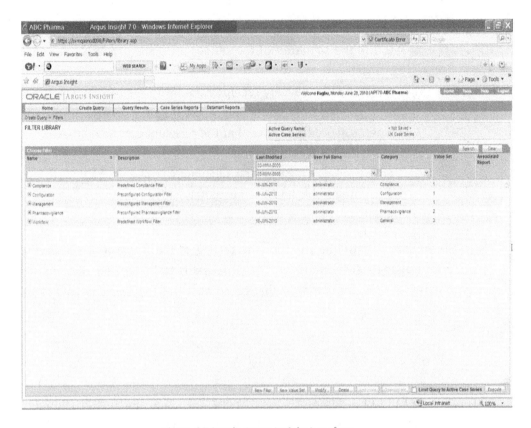

Figure 20 Oracle Argus Insight Interface

7.4   Possible options for implementation

There are a few possibilities for the implementation of the system. A possible solution is one where all modules are cloud based, that could be done by an external provider that is offering the service (public) and can be used by the organizations paying based on their utilization. Other possible solution is a model where the organization is the one that is offering the service like can be a private model that is created and managed by an organization like the FDA in their premises. As well there are options like community cloud models, where a few organizations decide to share the resources and use it accordingly, in this case different organizations like FDA and EMA decide to create a system that will be used by them and others and is completely managed by them, with the benefits of sharing resources. Other model is a mixture of the previous models, where for example, some modules are managed and maintained by the organization (private) and other using public systems like the use of a common gateway (public).

At this stage we will need a set of attributes or characteristics that will be measured and chosen in order to decide what model will be implemented. In order to have more information about the requirements of the system a table (table 2) with the requirements using the same model that ENISA (Catteddu Jan 2011) will be used for the description of the sample services in the implementation.

Characteristic	Attribute	Description
Data Sensitivity	Type of Data	Sensitive and Personal Data
	Information Security and resilience	Information Security and resilience: High Integrity, High Confidentiality, High Availability
Scalability	New services required:	Yes, in the future
	Volatility of the demand	High for the external users and sources of reports, especially in cases of specific issue with a drug.
	Anticipated storage requirements for the next 5 years	Predictable, using current trend
	Peak of concurrent users	High, especially for reports in case of an issue with a drug being detected and made public.
	Proportion of Data in active use	High, as all the past data is used for the current reports.
Service Reliability, availability and performance requirements	Availability required	99.99% (High)
	Unplanned downtime	Less than 1 hour
	Real-time response	Medium
	Performance online	Standard reports are generated between agreed timelines based on 100 concurrent users.
	Performance batch	process at least 50000 safety reports per hour
Collaboration and Interoperatibilty	Possibility of retrofit information from searches (itself or search providers like Google trends)	Yes
	Possibility of integration with current health online systems like Google Health	Yes
Identity, authentication and access	Identity Management	Identities of partners and users must be managed internally
	Credentials and	Credentials of partners and users must be

management	permissions provisioning for users	issued and managed internally, and must be verified before granting credentials.
	Role-Based Access Control (RBAC)	Yes
Encryption	Encryption	Yes during the transfer of the safety reports. It is recommended to encrypt the rest due to legal requirements
Legal and compliance	Data protection	Yes, applicable by law
	Access control	Both Mandatory access control and role based access control should be used.
	Accountability	Yes, by law
	Data location and legal jurisdiction	Yes, both by law

Table 10 - List of characteristics and attributes for a pharmacovigilance implementation

7.5   MMRF Phase 1 - Analysis

The implementation of the first phase will imply to do the analysis of the different options in which the MM System could be implemented. This will be probably the longest phase of the cycle when is executed the first time. Next times it will be faster as not a complete analysis will be done, but only changes to the current implementation. In this phase we will review the system to be implemented, and what are the main entities of the system, as well as different options for the interactions with cloud providers and using their services. It will imply to see what different options for cloud implementation will be taken into account and the decision of what is the most useful for this phase.

Regarding the utilization of different cloud architectures, three options are proposed. The first one is SaaS, in that case the system will be used as an application by all the main users and scientific administrators of the system, the provider/s (that can be the organization –private or an external providing that is offering the system -public) is the responsible of managing all the system and controlling and creating the business rules, and will charge per utilization of the application, the final users only will need to use the system remotely as a normal application. In the second architecture PaaS, the system has been developed using one of the current PaaS offered by the main vendors that have been chosen like Google App Engine or Microsoft Azure. In this case the system should be developed using these technologies. It will have an impact on the decision if there was a system before that will be migrated and what technology was used before for this system. For example, let's imagine that the system was developed using Microsoft .NET technology and MS SQL Server Database, in this case it will be easiest to create the system using Microsoft Azure as probably a lot of components could be reused with minimum changes. Using this architecture most of the characteristics like abstraction and specific cloud APIs of the cloud will be used. The last architecture is Infrastructure as a Service, in this case basically the virtual infrastructure of the provider is used to deploy servers and pieces of infrastructure, where could be new servers where the system in deployed or even the previous servers/system that are migrated to the provider using the same Operating system.

In table 5 some examples of for the model are described, the examples are based on the previous described modules. Because of the huge range of possibilities that we could have for implementing the system using the different architectures and models I have selected specific examples that will be used for describing each possible implementation so it will be easier provide more accurate information.

	Software-aaS	Platform-aaS	Infrastructure-aaS
Public Cloud	An external vendor implements the system with all the modules using a proprietary application for the web and business logic modules and some vendor's applications for the gateway and data mining modules. The proprietary application has been develop using a standard computing language (J2EE). The security module is implemented using a standard open source system. All the system is offered through a web portal where the users can log in using their credentials to the different modules. The system is offered to all registered organizations and is charged by user and number or reports. The vendor has all their system in one main datacentre that is their own datacentre in the US and they have a backup datacentre in the US with data replication. In a SaaS service there is less control of the system as we only see it as an application.	The organization that provides pharmacovigilance services deploys the system using Google app engine with Java. All the main modules are created using this system. But not all functionality is possible at this stage, specially the datamining / datawarehouse module. The security module is implemented using APIs for Google accounts. Data access has been done using datastores being a change in mentality for the developers. The application is deployed in a cluster on the Google datacentres that use master/slave replication between datacentres, all are public datacentres. The charging of the system by Google is done using custom budget on Google app engine rates based on Network traffic, storage and CPU. In this case there is more control of what is happening behind the scenes, but still are things like data location, data and application redeployment that is not managed by us.	The organization that provides the pharmacovigilance services deploys the system using an external provider that offers infrastructure services. The virtual servers of the organization can be deployed in the external provider (like Amazon). The system will be implemented in the same way as was in the previous company, with the same systems and modules. The DB can will be implemented using the DB Service offered by Amazon as well. The rest of the modules will be implemented using virtual servers in the new datacentre. The charging will be done using the normal Amazon charging services per CPU and storage. This is from the three models the one that offers more control as the application is running according to what we have decided; we still do not have control of the physical infrastructure.

	Software-aaS	Platform-aaS	Infrastructure-aaS
Private Cloud	Similar to the SaaS Public, but in this case the system is deployed internally and offered as a Service to users. Some people consider this option as a traditional model of an organization offering an application over the internet and charging per user. The organization that provides pharmacovigilance services deploys all the modules using a proprietary application for the web and business logic modules and some vendors applications for the gateway and data mining modules. The proprietary application has been develop using a standard computing language (J2EE). The security module is implemented using a standard open source system. The system is offered through an internal web portal where the users can log in using their credentials to the different modules. The system is offered to all registered organizations. The organization has all their system in one main datacentre that is their own datacentre in their premises and they have a backup datacentre in their DRP datacentre with data replication. More control over the system and data, but usually more expensive.	Similar to PaaS in Public, but in this case, the system is deployed internally on the organization datacentres. Some providers like Microsoft offers the possibility of deploying the system internally (MS Azure private cloud in a box, or Oracle Fusion Enterprise, or VMWare cloud foundry), but these solutions are quite big for small to medium companies to be deployed internally on most of the cases. So this is why in this case the solution is deployed most of the cases in community cloud models. For this case, the organization that provide the services has deployed these using vmware cloud foundry and using Java and springsource as the choice for the developer framework. As with the public model, the biggest drawback is that is not easy to implement all the functionality with these frameworks, specially the data warehouse module.	In this case the solution is simpler that in the previous cases. Basically the organization is using a technology that is providing the infrastructure that will enable the system administrators to deploy the servers in the internal datacentres. Products like Vmware vcloud, where usually the ICT department operates like a cost center and the department that is responsible for the pharmacovigilance application deploys the virtual servers and virtual devices into the platform and is charged by server and utilization. One of the big drawbacks is that with these models the elasticity is not as good as with the public models, as the number of servers that can grow is limited by the lack of economy of scale. In this case we have control of the physical infrastructure behind. From all the combinations, this is probably the one that offers more control.

	Software-aaS	Platform-aaS	Infrastructure-aaS
Community Cloud	Similar to the Private SaaS, but the main differences is that in this case the system is deployed by two or more organizations, looking for sharing costs and using economies of scale to reduce cost. The system can be managed by external or common company that charge to the organizations per user.	Similar to Private PaaS, but in this case the solution is shared by multiple organizations. The pharmacovigilance solution is deployed in a platform that is shared for different organizations. A typical case could be that two or more main organizations decide to use economies of scale and create a common platform using one of the current platforms like the vmware cloud foundry. This solution is taken in this case because is an open source solution.	In this case, as with the Private IaaS, the solution is an Infrastructure solution, but in this case is shared in order to have better economies of scales. This solution has the advantages form the point of view of IaaS that permits reusability of current systems without rewriting the code again, and from the Community solution that is shared and usually the elasticity is better and the cost as well due to the economies of scale.

Table 11 Examples of different models and architectures for implementing the system

As we can see from Table 11 Examples of different models and architectures for implementing the system, the combinations of possible solutions are infinite, I have not included the hybrid model, that will imply to have different modules or components using different model, like for example having a most of the modules in a private solutions and having the email service managed by an external provider. In fact purely almost all the models are hybrid solutions, as apart from some military or nuclear facilities most of the systems rely on connection with external systems. This is why we have not included the hybrid model, in order to simplify this for the study of the proposed model.

We will need as part of the input for this phase the previous diagrams of the system. For this system we will use the one provided in Figure 21. It will be used as well different information about the different types of cloud solution.

The original system is a standard local solution where the system is deployed in two different datacentres operated locally by the customer organizations. Figure 21 - Original system without cloud integration explains how the system is deployed and how external users/organizations that send safety messages and receive reports are connected over the Internet with standard protocols AS1, AS2 and AS3. The safety reports are consumed by the central system and analysis reports and alerts are created in the central system. The main system functionality is implemented as a set of clusters (DB, app and web). The system is behind a set of firewall clusters for protection with a set of rules to offer the different services outside.

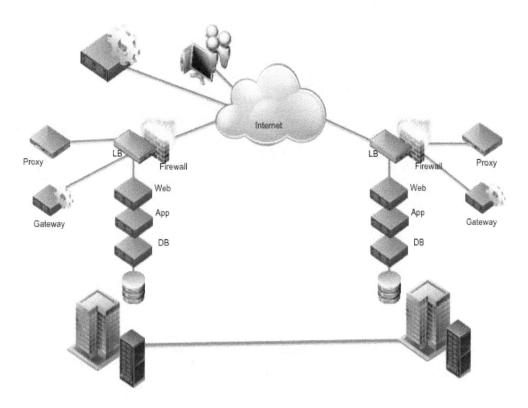

Figure 21 - Original system without cloud integration

7.5.1   Characteristics for each model

Once the different options are described, the next step is to define for the different models the characteristics, pros and cons of each model. Because of the great number of possible solutions (9 different models x 9 Characteristics) this has been divided into two main tables, one that explain the main different for the Public/Private/Community models (table 6) and other for the SaaS/PaaS/IaaS (Table 12 Characteristics and requirements evaluation by Cloud model). The characteristics that are studied are based on the requisites defined in the previous section used for the ENISA model (Catteddu Jan 2011). These have been studied for the Pharmacovigilance model. For this reason a scale of 1-5 is used for each value, being 1 the lowest and means that the model or architecture is not fulfilling at all the requirement, and 5 that can fulfil completely the requirement

	Public	Community	Private
Data Sensibility / Criticality	In this case the data is in an environment that is shared for multiple users and where the control is mainly on the provider. Usually the SLAs and agreements are fixed and cannot be modified due to the economies of scale of these companies. Value: 1	Similar to the Private model, the data confidentiality and integrity in this case is managed by a shared community, and depends on how the administration of this community has been arranged. There should be a trust between the members to assure the confidentiality; usually this trust comes from previous agreements or of working in same organization like the case of a government community where all agencies share resources. Value: 3	This is the best model for providing control over the data confidentiality. We can decide how the data will be managed and where will be stored because the data and systems is controlled by us. Value: 5
Scalability	The level of scalability and flexibility in public is very high due to the size and scale of these organizations; as well the demand management is very good, as part of their business is in providing a good control of this demand. Companies like Amazon can provide hundreds on extra resources in seconds, this would be almost impossible for other models like private. Value: 5	In this case the level of scalability is higher than in Private, but far from the level of the Public ones, and in the same way for the demand management. This is due in part due to the fact that usually is easier to calculate the demand for a business that is known, this is even higher in the Private model as the business and demand patterns are better known. Value: 3	Scalability is the lower of the three. Usually the availability of resources is lower. Value: 1
Performance	The performance for the pharmacovigilance system will be impacted by the way the program has been written and the quality of the infrastructure and communications. For the Public, the performance will depend on both variables. Compare to the community and Private usually is a bit lower because on the other two the system can be optimized for running that system only, in the public, there should be standard systems and usually are competing with other systems from different tenants. Value: 2	The performance can be tuned for the pharmacovigilance systems and specific hardware or systems could be allocated if needed and agreed with other community members. Value: 3	In this case the performance can be fitted to the requirements, if the resources are available. As well due to the higher control the different modules can be modified to meet the requirements. Value: 4
Business	Linked to the reliability, usually implemented by provider with datacentres that are geographically distributed. If properly implemented the business continuity can be very effective. Value: 4	Similar to the private cloud, but because usually more resources and different organizations involved in the community is easy to implement business continuity. Value: 3	More difficult to provide business continuity services because of the lack of resources and the geographical distribution of the company. Value: 2

	Public	Community	Private
Interoperability	While only one public cloud provided is used, the interoperability is high as all the users and organizations will use the same provider. The issue is when needs to operate with different public providers as the standards are not set and not currently used. For the pharmacovigilance case as the main modules are in only one provider, the value is high. Value: 4	Defined according to the agreement between the different parties. The interoperability as with the private one is done using SOA services that defines how these services should be used. Value: 3	Usually the interoperability is not easy in private models, as each one will use their own ways of implement the system according to the requirements. Usually as with the community the interoperability is done using SOA services. Value: 2
Authenticati	It is difficult integrate something that is different of what the vendors offer. Value: 2	If there is an agreement with the different members of the community, is easy to implement Mac access control and identity manager. Value: 4	Because it is private, the organization decides what system to implement. Value: 5
Encryption	It is difficult to implement a key management system. Value: 2	Encryption can be implemented if agreed by members and private and public key can be implemented and managed relatively easily depending on the number of keys to manage. Value: 4	Encryption can be implemented if agreed by members and private and public key can be implemented and managed relatively easily depending on the number of keys to manage. Value: 4
Legal Compliance	Difficult to apply in public clouds. Usually public providers have datacentres located in different countries and continents. As well the level of logging and audit possibilities in case of an issue is very low. Some providers are starting to provide clouds based on Specific regions like EU or USA clouds. Value: 1	If there is an agreement and according to the requirements and possibilities of the members could be easy. Value: 4	Due to the level of control the organization can implement what is the best solution according to the legal requirements. Value:5
Reliability	One of the main characteristics of public cloud is the high availability and reliability. Due to the scale of these systems, all kind of measures (geo-replication, clustering, physical and environmental) are adopted in order maintain availability and reliability figures, in part because the business of these companies depends on these values and the security. Due to the size of these companies and the number of customers that have, these are targets for possible attacks. The use of other external services could affect the reliability. When an interruption of the service happens, usually the time to recover is lower that with the other two models, because of the number of resources. Value: 4	Will depend on the resources available, the control done by the organizations and the implementation for the pharmacovigilance system. Depending on how the system is implemented, sometimes high availability is possible and even geo-replication or geo-clustering when different datacentres are used. Value: 3	For the private one the control is higher of the solution, but the resources dedicated to the availability and reliability is lower than for the public model. Replication or clustering of systems is not always possible or is not done between different datacentres, only if the resources are available to do this. Value: 2
Setup	Low, pay per use and all infrastructure is there with almost no investment Value: 5	Cost is shared between community members, but still there should be some investment. Value: 3	There should be a huge initial cost for creating the environment. Value: 1

	Public	Community	Private
Operational	Operational costs usually are higher than for the other two models, even if the costs are shared, and there are economies of scale, the provider needs to pay the investment and get a margin.	The costs are shared in the same way as the setup costs. There are different models, like equal cost, or pay per number of users, etc. There is some economy of scales and in theory there is no margin for the provider.	Usually the Costs are a bit higher than the community due to the economies of scale.
	Value: 2	Value: 4	Value: 3

Table 12 Characteristics and requirements evaluation by Cloud model

The values assigned in the previous two tables are based on how the requirement is met with that model or architecture. The values have been allocated based on how the requirements are met and even if try to be impartial, there is no certainty that are correct because are based on judgement of an expert, but this is just to illustrate the model and get a table that can be useful for the pharmacovigilance system. For implementation of other systems a similar model can be follow by the organization taking into account the system that will be implemented.

	Software-aaS	Platform-aaS	Infrastructure-aaS
Data Sensibility /	Using SaaS there is a lack of control of the system, and this includes the data integrity and the confidentiality of that data. For these models, if dealing with external providers, only legal agreements or SLAs defining how the data must be managed are possible options to control. Value: 1	Similar to SaaS, there is a lack of control; the control is higher than with SaaS, but still being problems for knowing how the data will be replicated within the and who has access to that data. Value: 3	In this case the control is higher, and we can implement Encryption if needed of the data in the virtual infrastructure. An example will be to create a virtual machine with an Database and encrypt the content of the data as we manage the DB software. Value: 4
Scalability	The scalability and demand management for SaaS will depends on the infrastructure and that is supporting the service below, and the way the application and the systems have been developed. If the SaaS the scalability is usually good, because the system has been created with demand management as one of the requisites. Value: 3	In the case of PaaS, the scalability and demand management is good, in fact because the system has been develop using a platform that is using cloud services and these platforms provide a very easy way to scale, the platform itself is done to be very scalable. Value: 5	Is more difficult to scale in this case of systems, not the infrastructure part that is easy and depends on the provider, but on the application side. When these systems are selected is to deploy existing systems that does not need big changes to work in cloud, that means that in order for the application to scale, changes needs to be done that are normally not easy to implement. In the pharmacovigilance example the DB is using a normal DB product running on a virtual server, in order to expand it if the product relies on clustering storage will be difficult to implement with an out of he box virtual infrastructure. Value: 2

	Software-aaS	Platform-aaS	Infrastructure-aaS
Performance	The performance on the three architectures will depend on how the system is implemented. If we use the case examples for the SaaS the system has been develop taking the requirements into account and is running on specific platform fit for purpose for that system, so the performance must be good and according to the requirements. Value: 4	In this case the main problem is the use of a develop platform where the model has been created to give more importance to other attributes like scalability. Usually there are some restrictions in the use of the platforms that restrict what can be done related to the improvement of performance. As an example some SQL queries must be done using one table only, this will be fast if the data is needed from only one table, but slower when we need to prepare reports with data from different tables. Value: 3	Because there is more control that with the other two options, usually the performance can be improved here if the proper resources are allocated. For the model will imply to get better and bigger virtual devices. Value: 4
Business Continuity	Linked to the Reliability, depends on how the SaaS system has been implemented. Unless that the business continuity was included since the beginning in the design of the solution, is difficult to address it once the system is working. Most of the cases is based on standard business continuity methods that are used for other existing systems. Value: 2	The platform development framework provides by default clustering and replication that makes possible to provide business continuity services. Value: 4	Most of the main vendors provide the possibility of replicate the virtual environment to other datacentre, even in different countries if permitted by law. This is done at virtual infrastructure level. Value: 4
Interoperability	In SaaS the application is implemented to work on its own environment, and in order to provide interoperability with other systems specific Services needs to be created. Value:2	Usually all the main platforms provide APIs for interoperate with other existing parts of the platform or other modules that can be develop in the future, the interoperability is easy to implement. Value:4	By default most of the vendors do not provide interoperatibilty and needs to be created in top of the existing systems. In some cases is not even possible even to migrate virtual appliances between providers. Value: 2
Authenticatio	Depends on the implementation of the systems, if this was not included as part of the design and the vendor does not offer it, it will be very difficult to change it. Value: 3	This depends totally on what is provided by the platform. Almost all the platforms provide Authentication and access control, but usually is very simple and does not cover the requirements for this system. Value: 2	Because the software is installed and controlled is easy to define and implement the solution that will be used. Value: 4
Encryption	Usually is very difficult unless the provider has implemented it with design. Value: 2	Very difficult, most of the providers do not offer an encryption solution that meets the requirements of the pharmacovigilance system Value: 1	Can be achieved if is implemented by software in the virtual infrastructure. This will impact performance, but it is possible to implement. Value: 4
Legal	Difficult to change the system if the application does not meet the legal requirements. Value: 2	The main issue with PaaS will be the way the data is managed by some platforms, specially the way the data is replicated and the lack of control of these replications. Value: 2	If the data is storage in Virtual Servers or virtual devices and can be replicated, it is difficult to control where the replication is being done. Value: 3
Reliability	Less control that with other architectures, the reliability will depends on how the system has been implemented and in most of the cases the user does not know details about how the system is implemented and managed internally. Value: 2	In this case there is better understanding of the system and how it is implemented. The platform usually provides by default clustering and replication capabilities by default. Value: 3	The implementation is done normally by the client and has access to all the details about the how the system works and is maintained. This is the model that more control provides to the organization. Value: 4

	Software-aaS	Platform-aaS	Infrastructure-aaS
Setup Costs	Setup costs are low if using an existing Application offered by a vendor Value: 4	Setup costs are very high, as imply to rebuild the system using the new platform development environment. Value: 1	Low as we can move existing virtual servers or applications into the virtual infrastructure. Value: 4
Operational	Charged by utilization, if the number of users is high (like the case of the pharmacovigilance system) can be expensive Value: 2	Once the solution is develop and deployed the cost is usually per utilization of resources (bandwidth, cpu, storage) Value: 4	The cost is based on utilization of resources (bandwidth, cpu, storage) for all the virtual servers that we have. Value: 3

Table 13 Characteristics and requirements evaluation by Cloud Architecture7

Once that the comments and the values have been allocated the next step is to use these values together for calculate the final values for each combination of model and architecture; this has been done using an average to get the values for each requirement, and the result is Table 14 Characteristics and requirements evaluation by Cloud Model and architecture.

Characteristic/ Architecture	Public			Community			Private		
Model	SaaS	PaaS	IaaS	SaaS	PaaS	IaaS	SaaS	PaaS	IaaS
Data Sensibility / Criticality	1	2	2.5	2	3	3.5	3	4	4.5
Scalability	4	5	3.5	3	4	2.5	2	3	1.5
Performance	3	2.5	3	3.5	3	3.5	4	3.5	4
Business Continuity	3	4	4	2.5	3.5	3.5	2	3	3
Interoperability	3	4	3	2.5	3.5	2.5	2	3	2
Authentication and Access Control	2.5	2	3	3.5	3	4	4	3.5	4.5
Encryption	2	1.5	3	3	2.5	4	3	2.5	4
Legal Compliance	1.5	1.5	2	3	3	3.5	3.5	3.5	4
Reliability	3	3.5	4	2.5	3	3.5	2	2.5	3
Setup Costs	4.5	3	4.5	3.5	2	3.5	2.5	1	2.5
Operational Costs	2	3	2.5	3	4	3.5	2.5	3.5	3

Table 14 Characteristics and requirements evaluation by Cloud Model and architecture

The next step in order to take a decision will be to assign a weight value to the requirements and based on what is considering most important for the organization. I will use a scale from 1 to 10 in order to assign the weighting values for each requirement/characteristic. If for any reason like legal requirements one of the requirements cannot be made, that option is automatically removed from the table.

For the pharmacovigilance model the legal requirements can be met so there is no one model/architecture that we remove. Regarding the weights, the most important for this model are the Data criticality/sensibility due to the kind of data that is managed, and the Reliability, followed by the performance, authentication, and maintenance costs, so the values are assigned giving higher numbers to those characteristics. In a later stage these values can be changed to see the effect on the different solutions.

Characteristic/ Architecture		Public			Community			Private		
Model	Weight	SaaS	PaaS	IaaS	SaaS	PaaS	IaaS	SaaS	PaaS	IaaS
Data Sensibility / Criticality	9	9	18	22.5	18	27	31.5	27	36	40.5
Scalability	6	24	30	21	18	24	15	12	18	9
Performance	8	24	20	24	28	24	28	32	28	32
Business Continuity	7	21	28	28	17.5	24.5	24.5	14	21	21
Interoperability	5	15	20	15	12.5	17.5	12.5	10	15	10
Authentication and Access Control	9	22.5	18	27	31.5	27	36	36	31.5	40.5
Encryption	6	12	9	18	18	15	24	18	15	24
Legal Compliance	8	12	12	16	24	24	28	28	28	32
Reliability	10	30	35	40	25	30	35	20	25	30
Setup Costs	6	27	18	27	21	12	21	15	6	15
Operational Costs	8	16	24	20	24	32	28	20	28	24
TOTAL		212.5	232	258.5	237.5	257	283.5	232	251.5	278

Table 15 Final results with weighting applied to the requirements

In this case, and taking into account the weights that we have use for the model the best result with 283.5 is the Infrastructure as a Service in a Community cloud model, followed by Infrastructure as a Service in a private Environment. The result makes sense if we follow the logic of what we are giving more weighting and the requirements that we are measuring. For the Pharmacovigilance model we are looking for a solution that has high reliability, this can be achieved with IaaS if the applications that are installed on top of the infrastructure provide it; form the hardware point of view the reliability is very high. Other requirement is to implement strong authentication and access control, and usually this can only be achieved with private or community solutions, and using IaaS will permit to have a solution that could be implemented by us. Regarding the costs, the main issue for the pharmacovigilance model is the operational, and for this the community is better than the private one, as the costs are shared between the community members. The final figures will heavily depend of the values that have been assigned to each requirement.

In the case of moving a pharmacovigilance system to a cloud solution, more details should be taken into account. Even if we have decided that that best option is to use an IaaS implemented on a Cloud provider, things like support of the system, communication with other internal systems should be taken into account. Let's imagine that we decide to move the current pharmacovigilance system from the provider to a community solution based on IaaS. The solution currently offered by an intergovernmental organization and a few countries is migrated to use this model. They decide to have a community cloud system, and for this they use the datacentres of two of the organizations (to save setup costs). They will use these not only for this system, but also for future systems of all the organizations in order to have economies of scale, especially in the ICT support department.

Once this stage is finished we will have a representation of the system indicating what parts of the system will be implemented internally and what will use cloud services. At this stage we will have the definition of the dependability values that we will use, and information of these values for the internal parts of the systems (micro-dependability) and estimation for the external part in cloud vendors.

During the first phase the analysis of the system will be done. For this we will get the SysML diagram of the system if this exists, usually from previous implementations if is not a new system. We will indicate all the main interfaces of the system, particularly the ones with other external providers, like cloud providers. We will define the main entities of the system, in this case and as shown in the diagram will be simplified to the ones related to sending safety messages and showing the reports. We will use the previous diagrams and information about the expected cloud vendors if exists (or in case that we could get it from existing monitoring authorities). We indicate the current dependability values for these services in each entity. As an example, we can get a value of 99.8% availability for the send safety report service and a Mean time between failures of 8000 hours. We will do the calculations with the internal parts of the system (micro-dependability). We will have once finished the first phase the Diagram of the system SysUML with cloud interaction (interfaces) and the list of dependability expected values for each Service that will be used.

7.6   MMRF Phase 2 - Implementation

The proposed implementation of the system is a hybrid solution where a cloud provider operates the main gateway functionality and the rest of the system is operated internally. In this case the cloud provider could be a community cloud provider as the result from phase 1. Figure 21 - Original system without cloud integration and Figure 22 - Proposed solution with cloud integration explains the physical implementation of the main system. The internal system is divided in three layers and in two datacentres with replication between the datacentres. The replication can be synchronous using storage technology for replicating the file systems of the Databases and application layer shared files or asynchronous using a normal DB and file replication technology.

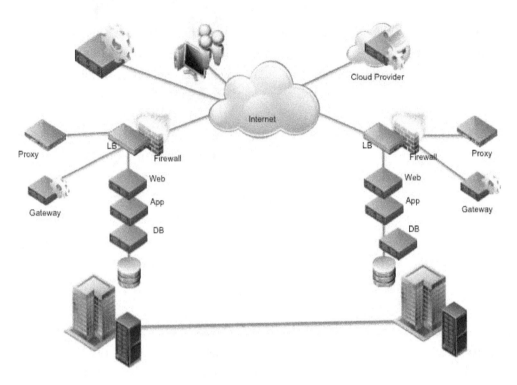

Figure 22 - Proposed solution with cloud integration

During the implementation phase we implement the proposed gateway in the selected provider, we will need to agreement the SLAs with the external cloud vendors.

The cloud provider (in this case a community cloud) will install a product that permits migration of the current system and have multitenancy for different systems using the same infrastructure. The migration will be done at the same time that a new version with new functionality is done, so all the test phase is done in the new datacentres. The benefit of doing it during the new release is that the old system will be operating normally and users will not be affected. All the requirements are implemented and tested in the new environment and support for the new system will be done in the new environment. The migration will not be very different form the migration in the old environment because due to the use of virtualization the same platform and development tools can be used.

Once the system is migrated and working, the system will be running on the new infrastructure, with the possibility of more resources on demand (more resources due to be a community cloud), there would be a rationalization on the use of resources as now the system is provided and supported by one provider, and the possibility of extend the use of these facilities to other related services. Regarding the reliability, could be better than with the previous solution, the time to fail can be reduced due to the best scalability of resources and time to recover can be increased as the support of the system can be rationalized (longer support frames, up to 24x7). As presented there are a many good reasons to change, but there are some risks as well that should be considered, like the agreement of responsibilities between the community members, how the support will be done and legal issues like who is the owner of the data, how should be managed, access to the data and many others that should be reviewed and agreed before migrating.

As we have seen this process can be used for helping in the decision of what model to use, for critical systems specific requirements and characteristics should be checked, and a proper risk assessment process for that system should be used. We can use a similar strategy for decide what cloud model and architecture to choose for any other system. Once possible area of investigation in the future is collect empiric values for each main characteristic and for each model/architecture based on real cases in order to have metrics that could be used in the future for choosing a specific cloud model and for helping with the process of the risk assessment.

Some of the outputs that will be produced on this phase are:

- List of entities with the detailed information of the interfaces
- SLAs expected values for the metrics
- Cloud providers with SLAs / WSLAs agreements of the cloud provider

Table Table 16 - Metrics expected values and results for Cloud Service GetSafetyReport for three different Cloud providers shows an example of one of the outputs of this phase. It shows the expected values for the metrics for the Service Get-Safety-Report offered by three different vendors.

Cloud Provider	Cost	Availability		Response Time		Time to Recover (in case incident)	
		Expected Value	Initial value	Expected Value	Initial value	Expected value	Initial value
Vendor1	900 €		99.999%		0.998 ms.		14 min.
Vendor2	800 €	99.995%	99.998%	0.9 ms.	0.894 ms.	2 min.	1 min.
Vendor3	700 €		99.995%		0.918 ms.		67 min.

Table 16 - Metrics expected values and results for Cloud Service GetSafetyReport for three different Cloud providers

Once the implementation of the MM System has been done and it is clear what parts will be provided by cloud services and how it will measured it is necessary to start with the part of the framework that will operate in the operation phase. This is the monitoring of the system.

It is necessary as well to define who will do the monitoring of the system; we will use a supervisor that could validate the data monitored.

7.7   MMRF Phase 3 - Monitoring

The next phase will be the monitoring implementation. We have selected the supervisor (in this case an existing external monitoring authority) that will be a monitoring authority and the monitoring entities that will check the selected metrics for the different cloud vendors. We have chosen for the ones explained in the previous Table 16. We have defined very basic rules for the micro and macro domains as well as the aggregation of monitoring values will be defined. In this case it will be the aggregated values of the monitoring authority for the Macro and a simple average for the micro.

7.8   MMRF Phase 4 – Review & improve

Once the monitoring is implemented and working properly we will review if the aggregation is working properly and the values are according to what is expected. We will compare the values to the ones forecasted before by the experts on the domain in order to confirm that are according to what is expected from the system. If the values are not as expected, we could change the cloud provider for a gateway interface.

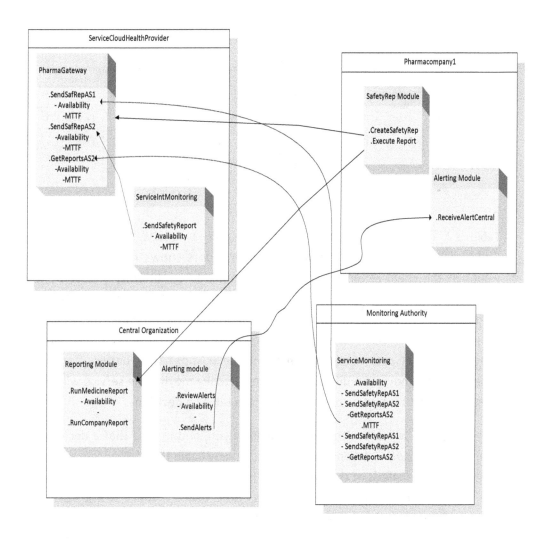

Figure 23 MMF simple representation of the system

Figure 23 shows a simple representation of the implementation of the system with the monitoring authority checking some of the Pharma Gateway services provided by the community cloud provider. The central legislative organization and the external pharmaceutical companies are using these services. Each of these organizations could have their own monitoring entities, but for some of the calculations for the metrics only the monitoring authorities will be used because it will be accepted by the cloud provider and the external customers as verified and valid information.

Cloud Provider	Cost	Availability			Response Time			Time to Recover (in case incident)		
		Expected Value	Initial value	Value Year 1	Expected Value	Initial value	Value Year 1	Expected value	Initial value	Value Year 1
Vendor1	900 €		99.999%	99.997%		0.998 ms.	0.954 ms.		14 min.	10 min.
Vendor2	800 €	99.995%	99.998%	99.999%	0.9 ms.	0.894 ms.	0.913 ms.	2 min.	1 min.	4 min.
Vendor3	700 €		99.995%	99.996%		0.918 ms.	0.984 ms.		67 min.	34 min.

Table 17 - Metrics expected values and Year 1 results for Cloud Service GetSafetyReport for three different Cloud providers

Table 17 - Metrics expected values and Year 1 results for Cloud Service GetSafetyReport for three different Cloud providers shows not only the initial values of the cloud services offered by the monitoring authority choose by the values after one year. Using this information and the rules defined for the MM system it can be review (even in an automatic way) the cost and the expected values for and decide whether to renegotiate the service with the current provider or in the case of not even meeting the SLAs or having better offers from other provider move to a different provider. Usually moving the service will imply to review it first by experts on the field before taking a decision.

This last phase will link with the first phase again, and in case that a decision to change the provider is taken it will imply to review again the MM system and start again with the analysis of the system and implementation and so on. Of course in the next stages this process will take less time because there is a lot of work already done from the previous cycles such as the definition of the interfaces, attributes, metrics and expected values for that metrics, as well as the definition of the rules that will be used.

7.9   Advantages of using the framework

The requirements that have been used for the justification of the different models in the previous state of the art have been reused and are explained below. The main attributes are explained for the pharmacovigilance implementation of the framework described in the previous sections.

7.9.1   Holistic Approach

The specified framework has a holistic approach, studying the system as a whole and taking into account as many parts of the system as required. It takes into account not only the internal part of the system as other models do. A very important part of the framework is to take into account the interaction with the external cloud services and to analyse what could be the impact of these services into the complete model. This has been described specially in the first phase of the framework where both the internal view and the external view have been taking into account with the help of the monitoring authority.

7.9.2   Micro Model

This framework can be used for Micro Models (low level of abstraction/ detail level is high), thus permitting the use of the framework for more detailed and specific scenarios. This has been proved as part of the phase one and two, the analysis and the implementation of the MM system.

7.9.3   Macro Model

As well can be used for Macro Models (abstraction is high/ detail level low), and combines both micro and macro models and be able to use them together to get better understanding of the systems, and be able to use more detailed data when there is the possibility. This is the case of the phases three and four where the data of the operational part of the system, specially the data of the services offered by external providers and the metrics of some of the attributes studied on these services by the monitoring authorities.

7.9.4   Operational phase usage

The framework can be used in the operational phase of the system, permitting to enhance the framework once the system is operational. In fact, phases one and two are used during the design and implementation phases respectively, but phase three and four are used during the operational phase of the MM system. It is very important as stated before when using cloud services where the information is not know in advance to use a framework that could be providing information about the system during the operational phase of it.

7.9.5   Action-based Feedback Auto

The framework can use feedback from how is working in real time to execute different actions automatically, providing the framework of a way to act directly into the system based on the information from the current subsystems, giving the possibility of improve the resilience of the system once it is in operation. The possible utilization of automatic actions based on predefined rules could permit the MM system to improve the way it works and adapt to changes in the services provided by the external providers.

7.9.6   Multi-source monitoring

As well the framework supports multiple-source monitoring; getting information from different sources, some of them validated by authorities to obtain monitoring values that can be used for the calculation of the resilience and reliability values. Anyhow, it needs to be clearly defined the aggregation rules for the monitoring if multiple sources will be used.

7.9.7   Automatic SLA

The proposed framework uses automatic SLA system to obtain and check the SLA values to confirm that are within the agreement and if not take automatic actions. Regarding the dependability mean, it is Fault prevention, fault forecasting and fault removal. The automatic SLA could be implemented using WLSA or other similar model for defining SLAs in an automatic way. In this framework most of the examples that have been used are based on the WLSA defined by Patel, but any other similar model could have been used.

7.10   Conclusions of the application of the framework

This section has explained an example implementation of the framework for a pharmacovigilance system where some parts of the system are provided by external cloud vendor. The application has been done from the theory point of view, and in the future it would be sensible to apply it in a critical system that could be implemented properly using cloud vendors. For have a complete testing of the framework there is the need to have monitoring authorities and proper standards for sharing the monitoring values. This could permit the reutilization of the models and information about different cloud services offered by different providers in a more wide way. The framework shows how the main characteristics that were used to compare the previous techniques and other different models are met when using the proposed framework. This framework is feasible from the point of view that can be implemented with not too much investment in new techniques or new technologies for systems that would like to use cloud services or move internal functionality to cloud services. As well the model is more efficient that using standard methodologies and methods for analyzing and evaluating the use of combined internal and external services, being the external normally provided by third parties and with lack of control about how these are provided. Using the MMRF framework both in the design operational phases and permitting to review the implementation of the MM system regularly permits having a new way of using and interacting with cloud services.

"Don't ask what it means, but rather how it is used."

[L. Wittgenstein]

8 Conclusions

The current fault models for studying dependability and fault analysis are not valid anymore for all cases, in part due to the complexity of the systems, it is not easy to get all the information about all components of the model and use one of the old models to find if a system will work properly, so system simulation or fault injections are other directions in dependably and fault analysis.

As a possible solution to this problem a framework is presented. The framework is based in the concepts of two different types of domains. One called micro-dependability that is used to define the boundaries of the system that are known and could be studied by the organization itself using the standard existing methodologies. The second is the macro-dependability and is used to explain the domain that is not known typically because it is not managed by us, but by an external cloud vendor and it is offered as external cloud services. The risk created in the macro-dependability domain could be inherit now by companies managing critical systems, including Critical Infrastructure services and they will not know the risks until probably is too late, as Egan described for the rafted networks (Egan 2007).

The proposed framework is based in a Deming do-plan-check/study-act cycle. The framework can be used for reviewing the dependability measures (availability, reliability, etc..) for a critical system using a combination of a Macro and Micro dependability domains. The MM system will have interfaces or be implemented in cloud services. The studied critical system has micro and macro dependability interactions. Micro with the internal organization and as part of other critical process or systems and macro because it uses external cloud services where only the main interfaces are known.

A very important part of the framework is the concept of the organizations, entities, the roles of each one, and the interactions. One of the most important organization types is the Authorities. It explains the creation of a standard network of monitoring authorities that could provide monitoring data about the services exposed by cloud vendors and could independently validate the results for each service. Currently there are some providers, normally monitoring providers that offer something similar, but this are still very immature and there is still a lack of standards that could be used by all vendors and customers in order to interchange this monitoring information about the operation status of these services. Some initiatives like WSLA (P. Patel 2009) have been created to solve this issue. These entities could monitor and validate not only standard values like availability or performance, but other values like reliability or resilience using specific mechanisms with the cloud provider without making this information public. Specific load tests, component failure simulation and security attacks could be done in a controlled environment by these monitoring entities. The information will be published and used automatically (WSLA) by customers in order to take decisions when these values change according to pre-defined rules.

The framework is implemented as a cycle, once the last phase has been finish and there is enough information to take decisions the decisions will be implemented together in a new phase one. The subsequent cycles will usually been more focused on the macro-dependability parts and especially in the interaction with the cloud services. Revision and changes in the micro-dependability, even if are less common, could happen in cases such as replacing some of the services provided internally for services provided by external cloud providers. The four phases are system analysis, system implementation, monitoring implementation and monitoring reviewing.

Having a concept of public model where data about different characteristics of the cloud services (dependability, security, availability, performance) could be validated with external authorities could simplify the use of these services by critical systems. Service Level Agreements still will be valid but will cover other characteristics that currently are not covered (resilience, time to recover, security) and could be validated automatically and actions could be executed (like change provider) based on predefined rules related to these attributes and costs.

The concept is not easy to implement, as this will imply a wide scale implementation of standards for monitoring and sharing data about systems with monitoring authorities. As well, it will imply to regulate the role of these Authorities, as currently there is not a common approach to share this data and provide it to customers that could be using it in operational time. Approach like WSLA defined by Keller (Keller 2002) and Patel (Patel 2009) could help to standardise this. There is still a long path to have something similar. But it is possible the only one if the use of these cloud services should be extended into other services like critical services, and the use of information as other utility (water, gas, electricity) is definitively adopted broadly.

The proposed framework and the concepts are used to provide a better understanding of the services that would like to be used in a cloud solution, showing the dependencies and how these affect the reliability of those services. The proposed framework has been presented to be used on ICT systems and mainly cloud solutions, but the model can be adapted for other type of ICT systems and even interaction with other non-ICT Systems, and the roles of producers/consumers and supported/supporting Infrastructure with other CIs like the Electric grid (Rinaldi, Peerenboom and Kelly 2001).

Before cloud services are adopted by an organization, and especially for critical systems or health systems, interdependencies should be reviewed not only for the organization that offers the service but also for the other organizations that act as providers for the one we will use. Once the risks are clear, the right cloud service and model can be chosen. And whatever solution is chosen, there should be plans in case of cloud service unavailability and a mechanism should be in place to provide service, even if it is a degraded service.

The next steps regarding the future work will be mainly in two areas, improving the current framework and developing a solution that could be tested. The second are will be testing it with a real system once the framework has been developed and implemented.

- Improve current framework:

    - Define with more metrics based on concept of Web Service Level Agreement defined by Keller (Keller 2002) and Patel (Patel 2009)

    - Using this in a combination with UML tools dependability models for graphical representation

    - Define aggregation rules for different monitoring entities

    - Define integration with standard reliability measures in micro

    - Define more attributes like maintainability (planned downtime), price and security and permit the use of more than one view (ICT, electricity,…).

- Test it for a real system that could be implemented in the cloud (pharmacovigilance)

8.1   Summary of the presented work

8.1.1   Introduction

Cloud computing and virtualisation have changed the way organisations are using ICT services (Ahrens 2010). Almost all types of organisations are starting to use cloud services, even for systems that can be classified as critical systems and Critical Infrastructures (CI) (Kenneth P. Birman 2011). As with virtualisation (Kroeker 2009), cloud services have been introduced in stages, starting with services that were not part of a critical system. There is a long list of reasons for using the cloud model such as elasticity, mobility, costs and the possibility for organisations to focus on their core business and treat ICT as the fifth utility (Rajkumar Buyyaa 2009). The main risk with this increased use is not what we see, but what we do not see. Complexity increases and new variables are introduced, in most cases, without the knowledge of the organisation that carries out the process. Egan (Egan 2007) uses the term "rafted networks" to describe systems that began simple and became very complex in an unplanned manner.

Due to increasing use, cloud-computing facilities will probably soon be considered to be a CI and should be protected as such. The interdependencies caused by these systems should be determined and the impact of possible cascade effects assessed. This section exposes some of the associated risks and suggests possible solutions for improving their visibility, thus enabling resilience to be improved. There are questions that arise from the use of cloud systems by organisations that provide critical services, for instance:

- How is it possible to assess the dependability, resilience and reliability of cloud systems when these are already used by our organisations?

- How can it be guaranteed that the availability figures will match the agreement with the cloud provider's Service Level Agreement (SLA)?

- What will be the impact on our systems if one of the cloud provider's services fails?

In order to answer these questions we have reviewed how existing frameworks cannot be adapted easily to cloud environments. We also propose a framework for analysing the dependability and resilience of systems when using cloud services. It is implemented as a cycle with phases where auto negotiation of SLAs and external monitoring agents are used to improve the resilience of a system relying on cloud services.

This section is organised as follows. The overall problem is outlined in section II. Section III presents some instances of the use of cloud computing in relation to critical systems, as well as some of the resilience related issues. Section V presents an overview of the state of the art. The proposed framework, including the concepts of *macro* and *micro dependability* (Diez O 2011), is presented and explained in section VI. The proposed framework and associated concepts do not aim to replace previous ones, such as *coupling* and *interaction* as defined by Perrow (Perrow 1999), but to complement them. No distinction is made between the different types of cloud models and architectures, making the framework valid for a wide diversity of cloud models. An example of the use of the framework is presented in section VII. Section VIII outlines some conclusions and future work.

8.1.2   Examples of Cloud computing services for critical systems

Most of the examples of uses of cloud computing in critical systems use the *Software as a Service* or *Infrastructure as a service* model. The details of these cloud-based models are not described here as this information is available in many other publications, such as "A view of cloud computing" by Armbrust (Armbrust, et al. 2010) or the Security Guidance from the CSA (CSA 2009).

Supervisory Control and Data Acquisition (SCADA) systems, Distributed Control Systems (DCS) and other control systems are found in industrial sectors and critical infrastructures. These are known under the general term of Industrial Control Systems (ICS). ICS are normally used in industries such as electrical (Kenneth P. Birman 2011), water, oil and gas. The reliable operation of these infrastructures depends on computerised systems and SCADA. In recent years different vendors have begun to provide solutions for integrating these systems with web dashboards that live in the cloud, as shown in Figure 24. The information collected by these devices can be viewed and controlled from different types of devices from different locations.

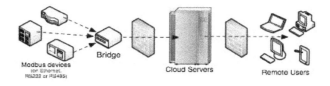

Figure 24 Example SCADA cloud integrator vendor.

Another example is the Department of Defence (DoD) Rapid Access computing environment (RACE). Robert Lentz (Lentz 2009), who is responsible for cyber security at The Pentagon, presented the benefits of private cloud computing for the DoD. To obtain these, the Defence Information Systems Agency (DISA) is testing a DoD-managed cloud-computing environment called RACE, which enables DoD users to access virtual services and storage from a web portal. DISA manages the IT infrastructure for 4 million DoD users and operates 14 datacentres around the world. The RACE portal (staff 2010) describes the system: "This quick-turn computing solution uses the revolutionary technology of cloud computing to give you the platform that you need today, quickly, inexpensively and, most importantly, securely."

IBM and FONAFE ("Fondo Nacional de Financiamiento de la Actividad Empresarial" of the Peruvian State) are working on the creation of a private cloud infrastructure for centralising the IT operations of 10 government bodies that provide critical services like transportation, electricity, post and ports in Peru (IBM 2011). This includes the consolidation of 10 datacentres, using an outsourced model based on private cloud. The purpose is to reduce costs and improve efficiency.

Another case is provided by radio system for emergency services (SaaS). The purpose of this system is to allow the fire brigade, police, emergency management and other public agencies to interconnect their private push-to-talk radio (Lipowicz, Cloud computing moves into public safety 2009). These tasks are not executed in their local servers and instead are moved into shared datacentres accessed via the Internet. These agencies have realised several benefits, most of them related to the use of cloud systems. In particular, the low cost of entry of using these technologies; there is no need for a big investment in interoperability infrastructure, due to the pay-per-use model.

Nebula is an open-source cloud-computing project and service created by NASA (Shackelford 2011). It was developed to provide an alternative to the costly construction of additional datacentres. Nebula provides a simplified way for NASA scientists and researchers to share large, complex data sets with external partners and the public. The model is based on the open standard "OpenStack" for open source cloud computing that follows a similar model to Linux. It is based on two key components: OpenStack Compute is software for provisioning and managing large groups of virtual servers; and OpenStack Object Storage for creating redundant, scalable object storage using clusters of commodity servers to store large quantities of data.

As can be seen, in most of the examples the cloud services start by replacing the 'non-critical' parts of the system to become part of the critical in a later stage. The main reasons to move to these technologies are costs and improved functionality. We have seen that some systems that could be used for critical situations rely on cloud services, but cloud services are mainly created for providing standard services - services that are cheap due to the economies of scale, where resilience or reliability are not always the main drivers, but the costs are.

8.1.3   Definition of the problem

8.1.3.1   Terms definition

Cloud computing services, known also as *Infrastructure as a Service (IaaS)*, *Platform as a Service (PaaS)*, and *Software as a Service (SaaS)* deliver infrastructure, platform or software, all made available as subscription-based services using a pay-as-you-go model. These services are noted by Armbrust (M, et al. 2010): "Cloud computing, the long-held dream of computing as a utility has the potential to transform a large part of the IT industry, making software even more attractive as a service".   In this section we will define the problem of resilience when cloud computing is adopted for critical systems and infrastructures. First, we will try to clarify the "resilience" term.

Resilience is defined as the "ability to adapt to changing conditions and prepare for, withstand, and rapidly recover from disruption" (Risk Steering Committee. Department of Homeland Security 2010). It defines the ability of a system to provide and maintain an acceptable service level when challenges occur during normal operation. Berkeley and Wallace (Berkeley and Wallace 2010) apply the resilience concept to infrastructures, as the ability to reduce the magnitude and/or duration of disruptive events. Laprie (Laprie and LAAS-CNRS n.d.) defines resilience as the persistence of service delivery that can justifiably be trusted when facing changes like unexpected failures, attacks, accidents or increased load. According to Bouchon (Bouchon 2006) resilience is the potential to remain in a particular configuration and to maintain its feedback and functions, involving the ability of the system to reorganise following disturbance-driven changes. Another possible definition of a resilient system is one that can withstand a number of sub-system and component failures while continuing to operate normally. This is commonly achieved by adding redundancy, eliminating single points of failure during the design and proper maintenance. Kishor et al (Trivedi, Kim and Ghosh 2009) give more details of the definitions and possible uses of resilience in the computer industry, along with a comparison of different dependability metrics, such as availability, performance and survivability.

Kroger and Zio (Kröger and Zio 2011) define resilience as the ability of the systems to anticipate, cope with/absorb, resist and recover from the impact of a hazard (technical) or disaster (social). Garlick (Garlick 2011) describes how community cloud computing systems could be used instead of other types of systems (including other types of cloud) to improve resilience, especially in case of disaster, where the geographic distribution of community cloud systems is higher than for traditional systems. In addition, Madni (Madni 2009) does not focus on fault prevention alone, but describes how resilience-engineering focuses in building systems that are able to evade accidents through anticipation and survive disruptions through recovery and grow through adaptation.

8.1.3.2   *Risks related to resilience and dependability in Cloud*

A great risk associated with Cloud technology use in critical systems and infrastructures is the lack of awareness of the extensive interactions and interdependencies between the components of critical systems. As described previously, the use of cloud computing as the new utility is commonly adopted by small organisations, where ICT departments are expensive to maintain. We struggle to envisage the idea of a nuclear plant, a medical device or health service using cloud services for critical parts of its infrastructure. However, a few years ago the same was true of virtualisation technologies, because of their inherent technological complexity, but now they are widely used in some of these systems, e.g. the use of virtualisation on medical devices to accommodate different systems running on the same device.

We could consider that this problem is not currently happening or is sporadic, but it could soon happen that the criticality of the systems using these types of services grows in the near future. This means that the possible impact of these new models should be taken into account. For example, what could happen if part of the control of an electrical grid is managed from a cloud service and this service fails?

One issue is how to keep the same quality attributes when we add cloud services to the complexity of the system. Another is that, over time, more and more organisations will use cloud services so the intrinsic criticality of these services will increase (Egan 2007). Consequently, cloud providers and services will become a Critical Infrastructure too. There is a hidden risk for organisations, mainly because there is insufficient control over which systems could be affected in the case of cloud services outage. Furthermore, it is not easy to reuse one of the existing models implemented in other engineering areas because of the complexity of the cloud systems and the lack of data due to the secrecy of cloud providers. For instance, it will be very difficult to get all the necessary information from a vendor such as Amazon or Microsoft Azure to use a Markov chain for assessing reliability (Rahul Ghosh 2010). Mainly due to the fact that most of the information regarding internal design and operation of these services is dealt with as their competitive advantage.

In conclusion, it is clear that there is an important problem, namely the vulnerability of complex systems associated to their increasing reliance on cloud services. This problem applies in a similar way to (i) cloud services themselves and (ii) how they are used in critical systems. So far the problem has been viewed in terms of dependability; however, it would be better to consider it now from the resilience point of view.

8.1.3.3   *State of the art*
In this work the term resilience is used to describe a characteristic of cloud systems. However, when analysing cloud systems, reliability has been historically the main concern. There are many reliability models for computing systems, adapted to different situations and environments. There are different ways of approaching the issues of dependability and reliability in cloud environments, for example, modelling and simulation techniques. Modelling techniques with a strong mathematical foundation, such as Stochastic Petri Nets or Reliability Block Diagrams (Malhotra 1995) can also be used to evaluate dependability for cloud computing. The current models used for reliability and dependability of cloud systems are based on standard reliability and dependability models used in computing systems. There are reliability models for distributed computer systems and grid computer systems that could be used for cloud computing.

From the realm of distributed computer systems, Pierre & Hoan (Pierre 1990) define a two level structure where the first level is the backbone or communication sub-network and at the second level are nodes or terminals. The distributed software reliability in a distributed computing system is the probability of successful execution of a program running on multiple processing elements, where it needs to retrieve data files from other processing elements. The model takes into account all the programs that run in the different nodes. There are tools based on this concept using *Minimal File Spanning Trees (MFST)*, like the analytical one presented by Kumar et al (V. H. Kumar 1986) and that are used in homogenously distributed hardware/software systems. Kumar et al later proposed a faster algorithm for reliability evaluation.

Kumar & Agrawal (A. a. Kumar 1996) introduced a "Distributed Program/System Performance Index" which can be used to compare networks with different features. Other concepts, such as the *Analytical Hierarchy Process (AHP)* have been used for the evaluation in distributed computing environments; for example the one presented by Fahmy (Fahmy 2001) is based on Markov reward models. Yeh (Yeh 2003) has extended the distributed systems reliability model, using a multi-state concept.

The reliability calculation must consider the resource management system, the network, software and any other components. Markov modelling is normally used to evaluate the resource management system.

Malek (Malek 2008) explains how the classical reliability assessment approaches are mainly suitable during the design stage for comparative analysis of different design options, but not for online assessment and short-term prediction. Instead, he proposes runtime monitoring for dealing with dynamic systems. It is more difficult to forecast the actual system runtime behaviour during the design and development phase.

Nevertheless, the models used for distributed computer systems are not always valid for cloud environments. The main problem is that these models are based on processes running on distributed nodes in order to share the computing functions among the hosts; in most cases these are homogeneous distributed systems or centralised heterogeneous distributed systems (Dai 2003). These models could apply to the internal functioning of most cloud technologies, in what will be described later in this work as *micro-dependability*, but not to more complex cloud scenarios due to the complexity of the systems and different types of interaction between providers and consumers.

Another type of reliability model is the one for grid computer systems. In this case, and in a similar way to cloud computing, there is large-scale resource sharing and wide-area program communication. As with cloud systems, it is difficult to analyse the grid reliability due to its highly heterogeneous and wide-area distributed characteristics. Foster et al. (Foster 2002) described the basic concepts of the grid and presented a development tool that later became Open Grid

Services Architecture. Cao (Cao 2002) presented a grid computer agent-based resource management system that uses quantitative data regarding the performance of complex applications running on a local grid resource. Xie and Poh (Poh 2004) define grid program reliability as the probability of successful execution of a given process running on multiple virtual nodes and exchanging information through virtual links with remote resources.

From the literature, it is clear that the presented models are based on traditional dependability models, including traditional information systems reliability models. Some of these models (M. Xie 2004) are not valid for cloud computing, mainly because of the complexity of cloud systems and the lack of information, as discussed. We will now present alternative models that are better for reliability of information systems. Those models, however, will also be criticised for its lack of ability for dealing with cloud systems.

A. Dai et al. Holistic Cloud reliability model

This cloud model takes into account a holistic view of the cloud service. Dai et al. (Yuan-Shun Dai 2010) classify the possible failures in two categories, depending on when the failures can occur. The algorithm evaluates the overall cloud service reliability in the execution phase. It is necessary anyhow to have detailed information, including execution times for all elements. A clear design and knowledge of all parts of the model is also essential. This is not always possible for cloud customers.

B. Abbadi Operational Trust for clouds

Imad M. Abbadi (Abbadi 2011) proposes assessing operational trust for cloud services. Abbadi defines a set of properties that establish the trustiness of a cloud service. The proposal can be used for evaluating properties like reliability without the need for information on the internal operation of the cloud system. This model does not present a way to automatically interact and react to the information that generates. Neither is there a clear definition of how the information is collected nor how different sources of information can be merged when values come from different vendors.

C. CloudSim

Calheiros et al. (Calheiros 2011) propose a repeatable simulation approach for the evaluation of several cloud service attributes, such as performance, under varying system and user configurations. They propose to use an extensible simulation toolkit (CloudSim) that enables modelling and simulation of cloud computing systems and application provisioning environments. CloudSim takes a holistic approach, giving the possibility of taking into account different infrastructure and services in the model. However, it is based mainly on the resource-provisioning model. It can be used for low level and high level modelling, but it is not designed to be integrated with operational environments nor can it apply actions based on SLAs or predefined rules.

D. Lin and Chang reliability for a cloud computing network Patent

Yi-Kuei Lin and Ping-Chen Chang have a patent (Chang 2012) for the estimation method for reliability evaluation of a cloud-computing network. It focuses on measuring the reliability of the cloud service's network infrastructure. It uses a model of the network and assigns a maintenance cost to each edge (network connection or physical cable). It permits finding the reliability of the network of a specific cloud system, but does not include the integration with different types of systems and cloud vendors. It can be used during system operation, once it has been deployed in production.

E. Almahad et al. SLA Framework for cloud computing

Almahad et al. (Alhamad, Dillon and Chang 2010) define the use of dynamic SLA metrics for different groups of cloud users. They define SLA metrics for IaaS (e.g. response time), PaaS (e.g. scalabiliy), SaaS (e.g. reliability) and Storage as a Service (e.g. system throughput). They also define general SLA metrics that can be used for any type of cloud service (e.g. support, security). This framework could be used in a holistic approach as it could be used to monitor and retrieve metrics from different parts of the system and the system as a whole. However, the framework does not define a way to amalgamate information from different systems and vendors.

F. Gustavsson and Sta SLA for Critical infrastructures

Gustavsson and Sta (Gustavsson and Stå hl 2010) introduce the concept of using cloud services for Critical Infrastructure, in particular for smart grids. They explain the difficulties of using very complex and dynamic systems and the challenges of controlling them when used in Critical Infrastructures. They introduce the use of SLAs as mechanisms of high-level co-ordination between the different stakeholders and monitoring of regulatory policies. The model concentrates on the smart grid, and does not have a holistic approach for cloud systems.

G. Xu and Wang co-operative monitoring for Internet Data Centres

Other approaches are focused on the use of empiric data, mainly from monitoring, and they use this data together with information from other models. Xu and Wang (Wang 2008) define co-operative monitoring for Internet data centres. It uses an algorithm for locating monitor nodes for the purposes of load balancing and resilience. The benefits of this model are that the monitoring load is shared; this makes it more resilient than normal centralised monitoring approaches, but it primarily describes how to load balance monitoring, not in what to do with values obtained.

H. Park et al. monitoring service for fault tolerance in mobile cloud

Park et al. (JiSu Park 2011) use a Markov chain based monitoring service to help improve fault tolerance in mobile cloud computing. It analyses and predicts resource states, making the cloud system more resistant to faults caused by the unpredictability of mobile devices. This technique could be used to solve some of the reliability problems already presented. The model concentrates on mobile devices that use cloud services because these devices are considered unstable. It does not take a holistic approach, as it only considers mobile devices. It is mainly used for collecting information about the system, monitoring specific metrics to improve the system.

I. Song Fu framework for autonomic anomaly detection in the cloud

Another approach is the one presented by Song Fu (Fu 2011) that defines a framework for autonomic anomaly detection in the cloud. Information from different nodes is used to measure the relevance and redundancy among the large number of performance metrics available. The approach of using data from monitoring systems and predicting what it implies is similar to the one presented in this work. The framework uses a semi-supervised decision tree detection mechanism and only the most relevant metrics are used to identify anomalies in the cloud. It focuses on the selection of metrics and cannot be used for SLA measurement or to take automatic actions based on the metrics.

J. Pietrantuono et al. online monitoring of system Reliability

This monitoring approach (Pietrantuono, Russo and Trivedi 2010) gives an estimate of the reliability of the system in operation, which is compared with the expected reliability. This approach combines traditional reliability modelling with dynamic monitoring and analysis when the system is in operation by periodically evaluating the system's reliability trend. Once the system is operational, they calculate the runtime reliably and an alarm is triggered if it is lower than expected. The model encompasses only a single system and focuses mainly on the reliability of the components.

K. Undheim et al. cloud SLA availability model

These authors (Undheim, Chilwan and Heegaard 2011) define an overall availability model for a cloud system and explain the need for a better definition of the KPIs (Key Performance Indicators) used for availability, taking into account network availability. It explores how SLA related KPIs for cloud datacentres and vendors are calculated and how they can be improved. According to the authors, KPIs should be available on demand and SLAs should be able to be adjusted on demand. Two of the possible factors that differentiate cloud services are the ability to deploy applications in different physical locations and the possibility for different applications to have different fault tolerance schemes.

8.1.3.4   Conclusion of the state of the art

Traditional models for studying dependability and for fault analysis are not always valid for cloud services. This is in part due to the complexity of the systems. It is not easy to obtain information about all components of a particular cloud service. System simulation and fault injection are other approaches that are being tried for dependability and fault analysis, but still are difficult to apply on these types of services.

The existing dependability assessment models and frameworks can be useful during the design phase of a system with cloud computing. Early approaches using statistical models likes the ones based on hardware, or the ones relying on component-based-systems that use the reliability of each component do not adapt well to the new architecture models like cloud computing mainly because the complexity of the systems and the lack of knowledge of the cloud systems' details by the customers. Previous models do not consider the influence of the system usage and the execution environment.

In conclusion, none of the current models and frameworks presented solves the proposed problem. Some of them rely on previous data to be used for the model, others focus in systems where the level of detail is high, but the level of abstraction is low; and others in the opposite, but not permitting to combine both, thus not solving the problem of evaluating the resilience and reliability of systems interacting with cloud services where not enough data of those services is known. As more cloud automation and dynamic selection of cloud services is becoming common, it makes sense to move to models that can be adapted to the operational phase. This will allow more dynamism to the systems that make use of the services provided by different cloud vendors. These models could make use of runtime monitoring and prediction, taking into consideration both quantitative and qualitative information derived from the cloud service actual usage. For this reason there is a need of a new framework that can be used for the study and analysis of the resilience, reliability and dependability of cloud services, and that applies to different cloud vendors.

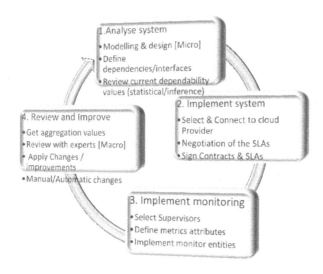

Figure 25 - *Phases of the MMRF Framework*

8.1.4   Macro and Micro Dependability Framework

As a possible solution to address the need mentioned in the previous section, a framework is proposed. Figure 24 presents an overview and outlines its phases, which will be explained later. The framework is based around two different domains. The first will be called *micro-dependability* and it is defined by the boundaries of the known system. The system owner, using existing standard methodologies can study it. An example will be an internal system that is provided entirely by the organisation with no dependencies in external providers (like the control IT system of a factory).

The second is *macro-dependability* and encompasses services supplied by external cloud vendors from which little information may be available, making existing methodologies difficult to apply. Risks within the macro-dependability domain could be inherited by organisations managing critical systems, including Critical Infrastructure services. These risks may not be revealed until disaster strikes, as Egan described for rafted networks (Egan 2007). An example is a system that has connections and dependencies in other external systems like the control system of the electrical network grid.

In the remainder of this section, the framework is presented: first, the elements (organisations and entities); second, the cycle process; third, the macro and micro dependability rules; fourth, he associated metrics and finally, macro and micro interactions are considered.

8.1.4.1   Elements of the Framework

Very important parts of any framework are the constituents used in it. In this case, the main concepts are the organisations and the entities, including their roles and possible interactions.

An *organisation* is any corporation that will be part of the system. Each organisation can have different type of entities. The main organisation types are:

• Providers (e.g. Amazon): This term is used for organisations that provide services. Normally they will be cloud providers.

• Customers: organisations that consume services offered by the Providers. In some cases the Customers can supply services to other organisations (such as service providers). Customers connect to Supervisors to get information about the services they use.

• Supervisors: organisations that monitor Producers and aggregate data about the different services offered. These can be public organisations or commercial ones.

Entities can be Producers, Consumers, or Monitoring bodies and an entity can have more than one role. The main entity types are:

- •Producer: offers infrastructure or software services. Services should have well defined properties or qualities. For example, a number of virtual CPUs or the behaviour of a software interface.

- •Consumer: requests and uses services from Producers. Most organisations, customers or providers, have Consumer entities because they use the services of Producers.

- •Monitoring entity: responsible for monitoring services according to the metrics defined for each service, usually associated to SLAs.

Each entity has attributes that define how it operates and its associated reliability/dependability. These attributes should be simple to describe and it should be possible to validate them by monitoring. Multiple Monitoring entities can be used to increase confidence in the attribute values. Supervisors provide independent Monitoring entities that supply data on the services provided by cloud vendors. This is an immature market and there are no agreed standards that can be used by all Providers and Customers to exchange monitoring information. Some initiatives like the Web Service Level Agreement (P. Patel 2009) (WSLA) have been created to try to solve this problem. These entities could monitor and validate not only standard values like availability or performance, but other values such as reliability or resilience using methods specific to each cloud Provider. The details of the infrastructure and services monitored need only be shared with Supervisors. Specific load tests, component failure simulation (Robinson and Higton 2007) and security attacks could be done in a controlled environment by Supervisors' Monitoring entities. The information will be published and used automatically by Consumers in order to take decisions when these values change according to pre-defined rules.

The consumer can be an external organization that is acting as a consumer of both services of the cloud community provider. In this example, a pharmaceutical company needs to send Safety reports and request Clinical Trial approvals. There are two types of interaction or connections between the entities: the dotted line that is used for monitoring of services (it should indicate the monitoring interval), and the continuous lines, used for expressing the real use of services from a consumer to a provider. If needed, more detail can be added by exploding the links. These services are consumed by other cloud organizations because secure email services are not the core business of the Pharmacovigilance cloud community provider that is specialized on pharmacovigilance services only.

Subsequent cycles will usually be more focused on the macro-dependability domain and especially on the interaction with the cloud services. As a result of phase 4, services may be moved between domains. The four phases are: (1) system analysis, (2) system implementation, (3) monitoring implementation and (4) monitoring reviewing.

Allowing data about cloud services (dependability, security, availability, performance) to be validated by Supervisors could simplify the use of these services by critical systems. This framework could be applied to other characteristics (e.g. resilience, time to recover, security) that are not normally included in SLAs. They will be validated automatically and corrective actions taken, if required, according to pre-defined rules. However, validation of the characteristics and automatic actions are not easy to carry out, as it implies a wide scale implementation of standards for monitoring and data sharing. Approaches like WSLA defined by Patel (P. Patel 2009) could help to standardise this. It may be necessary to regulate Supervisors if their services are to be trusted. The role of the supervisors is very similar to the one of the Certification Authorities (CAs) used for issue and validates digital certificates. However, in a framework such as this one it may be essential if the use of cloud services is to be extended to critical systems and for information technology to truly become a utility service.

The proposed framework helps to provide a better understanding of the use of cloud services. It shows dependencies and how these affect the reliability of services. The framework as presented is intended for use with IT systems that use cloud services, but it can be adapted for other types of IT systems and it could even include interactions with other non-IT systems, such as electrical grids (Rinaldi, Peerenboom and Kelly 2001).

8.1.4.2   Framework cycle process

This proposed framework cycle is inspired by Deming's do-plan-check/study-act cycle (Deming 1986). Resilience measures (availability, reliability, etc.) for critical systems can be assessed using a combination of macro and micro dependability based approaches. It is supposed that the object system depends partly or entirely on cloud services. The cycle is formed by four different iterative phases:

1. System analysis: In this phase we will review the system to be implemented, and entities, the main roles of the different parts of the system, called entities. If the system were a new one, there would be a design and development process as part of this phase. We should define the dependencies of the system as well as review target dependability (reliability/availability/resilience) values for the system. Once this stage is finished we will have a representative architecture of the system (e.g.SysUML) indicating which parts of the system will be implemented internally and which ones will use cloud services. At the end of this stage we will have the definition of the attributes that will be used to measure the system, and information of these attributes for the internal domain of the systems (micro-dependability) and estimation for the external domain in cloud vendors.

2. System implementation: Implementation of the proposed system is carried out, including connections to the cloud vendors that had been chosen in the previous phase. Part of this phase will imply the signature of contracts and definition and agreement of the SLAs with those external cloud vendors, for the Macro-dependability dimension. The different software agents that will provide the monitoring and SLA evaluation will be deployed and configured in this phase during the first cycle.

3. Implementation Monitoring: Until this phase, the design and implementation of the system will not differ too much from a traditional way, except the cloud-related aspects. In this third phase we will define and select the supervisor and monitoring entities that will check the selected metrics for the different cloud vendors. It is here when the different rules for the micro and macro domains as well as the aggregation of monitoring values will be defined.

4. Review and Improve: Once the monitoring values are implemented and working properly is time to review if the aggregation is working properly and the values are according to what is expected. Domain experts can review these values in order to confirm that they are according to what is anticipated from the system. There is the possibility of applying automatic changes to the system based on the values of the monitoring entities, for example changing a cloud provider for a specific interface if the values are not within the expected range.

The framework is implemented as a series of cycles. Once the last phase has been finished and there is enough information to make decisions, these will be implemented together in a new cycle, as a new phase one. The subsequent cycles will be more focused on the macro-dependability parts and especially in the interaction with the cloud services. Revision and changes in the micro-dependability, even if they are less common, could happen in cases such as replacing some of the services provided internally for others provided by external cloud providers.

During phase one, and as part of the definition of the services there should be included the attributes and rules that will be applied for these attributes. When calculating the dependability and its different characteristics like resilience, reliability, availability we will need to take into account type of domains and rules that will govern those domains. The micro dependability will be used as explained before for systems that are known and where traditional models can be applied.

8.1.4.3   *Macro & Micro Dependability Rules*

During phase one, and as part of the definition of the services, the attributes to check and the rules that will be applied need to be outlined. When calculating the dependability and its different characteristics like resilience, reliability or availability we need to take into account type of domains and rules that will govern those domains. The micro dependability will be used as explained before for systems that are known and where traditional models can be applied. But when working with part of the systems where we do not have complete information about how it works or how it behaves in specific situations, like for example a cloud vendor we should use what we defined as macro dependability rules, and values needs to be calculated in a different way.

As part of the phase one for each entity, when these are defined, the definition of the Services that the entity will provide should be included. The definition of the Service will be done differently depending of the type of domain:

- For macro domains (defined by external organisations) the Service and attributes: by Provider (of the producer entity). The Metrics and values: by Supervisors (Monitoring) based on Attributes defined in Producer entity by the provider.

- For micro domains (defined by the customer, internal organisation): Service, attributes, metrics and values defined by producer entity.

Another important aspect is when different attributes may be aggregated. For instance, if we are calculating the reliability of a cloud service that is composed of different other services with different reliability values. In order to calculate an overall value we must aggregate the other ones. Regarding this aggregation of monitored values from different sources we could point out the following:

- For macro domains: It must be done by Supervisor (monitoring entity), depending on metric and based on a weighted average. The supervisor entity will allocate different weights and do the aggregation.

- For micro domains: It is not always needed, only internal. If needed, the customer will aggregate them.

The last part of the process is the publication of the results of SLA achievements:

- Supervisors (Monitoring entities) do this part in Macro domains. Web dashboards could be used with results for each provider SLA achievement and optionally cost.

- For micro domains this is optional, as normally these will not be published.

Adding new consumers will be done in the following way:

- In Macro domains the customer should adjust monitoring metrics or get monitoring entity from monitoring supervisor (cost). Also assign weighing for new customer/consumers in monitoring entity.

- In micro domains adjust current internal metrics to be in line with macro metrics, such as values calculated with other techniques (RBD, FTA).

8.1.4.4   *Attribute Metrics*

It is important to define correctly the metrics that will be used in order to measure the attributes. These could be used as well for create the SLAs that will be agreed with the provider and in order to monitor if these SLAs are met. In this work the metrics are focused on the dependability, resilience and reliability, but others that could affect directly or indirectly should be added in a real scenario (cost, legal, security, etc.). One service offered by a provider can have one or more attributes, and these can have one or more metrics. A few examples of the possible attributes and metrics used are:

- Service Availability (Macro/Micro)

    o   Mean time between failures

    o   Incident rate

- Adaptability

    o   Mean time to discover an incident (MTTD)

    o   Mean time to invoke an action to remedy the incident (MTTI)

    o   Mean time to recover an incident (MTTR)

    o   Tolerance to attack

- Scalability (horizontal and vertical)

    o   Mean time to procure resources

    o   Mean time to deploy (MTTDp)

    o   Mean time to scale up (MTSU)

    o   Mean time to scale down (MTSD)

In order to measure automatically this information we use WSLA language defined by Patel (P. Patel 2009). Basically this will provide a mechanism to represent what will be monitored and control that is according to specific values that we have been agreed. The following structure is an example of the definition of the metric by Monitoring Entity SOSMonitoring1: How many Values (in %) of a Utilization Time Series are over a threshold of 90%:

```
<Metric name=OverloadDef" type="float" unit="Percentage">

    <DefinedMonitorEntity>SOSMonitoring1</DefinedMonitorEntity>

    <Source>Ymeasurement</Source>

    <Function xsi:type="MetThresold" resultType="float">

            <Schedule>BusinessDay</Schedule>

      <Metric>UtilizationTimeSeries</Metric>
```

```
<Value>

    <LongScalar>0.9</LongScalar>

</Value>

</Function>

</Metric>
```

The WSLA language is based on XML and could be extended to incorporate other functionality like rules for actions based on the expected values of the metrics and what can be done if these are not met.

8.1.4.5   Macro and Micro Dependability interactions

Micro interactions occur within the micro-dependability domain and macro interactions within the macro-dependability domain, where only the main interfaces are known. The micro-dependability interactions follow rules that are clearly defined and can be obtained using the traditional methods for dependability calculation. Rules could be simple calculation of resilience or reliability for a web cluster based on the number of concurrent servers and geographical location. Once these interactions are recorded, it will be easy to track dependencies of one service to other, as well as to monitor them. The interactions between different systems from different organisations define the macro-dependability ones. One of the issues related is the problem of representing the information about the dependencies of a cloud provider, mainly because usually providers do not disclose this information, considered by them as part of their know-how. One advantage is that when disclosed, the supervisors can have this information, keep it, validate it and updated. In this way they can offer this information to consumers in order to check the different values of the attributes during the first two phases before choosing a provider. This could be extremely useful for critical services.

8.1.4.6   Agents Implementation in the Framework

As explained in the previous sections, the framework used the different phases to get information about both micro and macro domains. In order to do that there are software agents that are distributed over the different entities. The agents are daemons/services that are running on the computer and implement the framework logic in four modules. These agents are defined for the supervisor, customer and providers. The main modules are:

- Definition: Responsible of maintain on the definition of the services, attributes and metrics and aggregation rules both macro and micro and the security information for each metric. This information is defined typically defined by XML schemas created by Supervisor organization in collaboration with Providers. These can be downloaded to the rest of Agents in Customers and Providers to maintain a common metric and rule base. At Supervisor level the aggregation rules are mainly macro and at Customers level the aggregation extra aggregation rules will be defined to aggregate macro and micro rules.

- Measurement: This module is responsible of executing the measurement of the metrics defined by the definition module. It will get the values for the metrics defined for each service and monitor them according to the designated time intervals. Providers have specific measurements that will be only used by them (such as clusterNetworkTroughput) for calculation of aggregation values (micro rules) and where only these aggregated values are exposed to the supervisors and customers.

- Aggregation: Module responsible of the aggregation of the metrics based on the rules (macro and micro). Applies the aggregation of the values based on the time intervals defined on the metrics and with the rule defined on the aggregated metric for that service.

- Reporting: This module shows information for each Provider/service/attribute/metric. It permits to group the information and represent it in different ways to take decisions during the phase 4 of the framework. An example would be the aggregate metric AverageResponsiveness of service GetSafetyReports provided by two Providers. We could get a report by the two vendors with the values of the last month of the metric together with the values of the cost by month of the service to help to decide what service to choose in the next cycle.

The agent's modules expose web services using a Service Oriented Architecture (SOA) (Zhang, SOA Solution Reference Architecture 2007) that can be used over http. Locally stores the information using xml on files or a relational database to store the information about attributes and metrics definitions, rules, and SLA aggregations.

8.1.5   Example of the use of the framework

For ICT departments running critical applications, understanding the implications of using cloud services is challenging. The proposed framework describes how the resilience of different cloud based systems mutually interact and influence each other and how is possible to monitor those interactions. In order to validate the framework, a case study of a generic pharmacovigilance system used by regulatory bodies is used. Pharmacovigilance systems monitor the adverse drug reactions of medicines and prevent possible harm for the patients. In order to do this currently governments all over the world collect safety reports of adverse drug reactions (ADR) from patients and healthcare providers using typically information systems. Once the reports are collected, they are processed and evaluated normally using data mining tools in order to find hazards associated with medicines and prevent future harm to patients.

Many departments do not even consider moving critical systems to the cloud, including health systems like the one proposed here. In our example, an actual critical health-related pharmacovigilance system is reviewed to decide on appropriate solutions for moving it to the cloud and to evaluate how these solutions can be implemented and assessed. This process can be applied to similar systems in order to get more information about what type of cloud model and architecture would be the best one, as well as to improve resilience while the system is in operation.

We considered three different architectures (SaaS, PaaS and IaaS) and three different models (private, public and community). Our focus has been the study of the reliability and resilience of the implementations, but due to its importance we included in the study other aspects like security, legal issues and cost.

8.1.5.1   Functional and Non-Functional Requirements

Some of the functional requirements of the proposed system, as described for a typical pharmacovigilance system (Mann and Andrews 2007), are:

- FR1: Supports multi-tenancy (country, legislation)

- FR2: Supporting both Human and Veterinary

- FR3: Reporting capabilities (including regulatory reports)

- Methods supported for signal detection:

- o FR4: Data mining capabilities (for a limited number of scientific administrators): extract meaningful, organised information, in this case signals, from large complex datasets. Will be used to identify hidden patterns of associations or unexpected occurrence in spontaneous reporting system databases

- o FR5: Case Series: evaluation of a series of case reports usually using specific algorithms that are commonly known. Proportional distributions, reporting rates, observed-to-expected analyses, case-control analyses, and survival analysis. Not all will be used, but at least one for this model should be used. In the future there should be the possibility to incorporate more and give reports based on different models.

- FR6: Use the ICH E2B standard (Use 2001) for data elements of safety reports

- FR7: Receive files from different options (mail, ftp, web) (AS1, AS2, AS3) and different sources (pharmaceutical companies, regulatory authorities, individuals and GPs)

  - o XML Files received will be validated using a template

  - o Acknowledge of accepted and rejected messages will be send

- FR8: Use of MedDRA (Medical Dictionary of Regulatory activities) Coding and ISO IDMP Standards

- FR9: Receive Clinical trials reports as well

- Optional functional requirements:

  - o FRO1: Possibility of retrofit information from searches (from itself or from search providers like Google trends)

  - o FRO2: Possibility of integration with current health online systems.

  - o FRO2: Include possibility of add business rules created by the scientific administrators for specific tenant.

Some of the non-functional requirements according to the standard non-functional requirements defined by ENISA (Catteddu Jan 2011) are:

- NFR1: Integration with other gateway software

- NFR2: Access to the system from any web device

- NFR3: Availability is more than 99.99%, and for the reliability we will try to minimise the mean time to failure.

- NFR4: Encryption of information and secure access with possibility of strong authentication

- NFR5: Response time is less than 0.9 for the GetSafetyReport service.

- NFR6: Time to recover is less than 2 minutes.

The main roles of the users are:

- R1: Safety evaluators

- R2: Scientific Administrators for the tenancy (country, countries)

- R3: ICT Administrators for the tenancy

- R4: Pharmaceutical companies

- Individuals

    - R5: healthcare professionals

    - R6: general public

8.1.5.2   Modules of the system

Main modules of the system are:

- **Reporting/Data mining module**. This module is used for reporting and data mining capabilities (for a limited number of scientific administrators): extract meaningful, organised information, in this case signals, from large complex databases and used to identify hidden patterns of associations or unexpected occurrence in spontaneous reporting system databases.

- **Rule Parses**: It crawls through the new safety reports in order to find patterns. Usually is implemented as services or daemons that run at specific intervals and connect to the database to get the data and process it. Permits the evaluation of a series of case reports usually using specific algorithms that are commonly known. Proportional distributions, reporting rates, observed-to-expected analyses, case-control analyses, and survival analysis. Not all will be used, but at least one for this model should be used. In the future there should be the possibility to incorporate more and give reports based on different models.

- **Web access module.** Will allow access to the system using a web browser. It permits to execute certain functionalities through a web interface.

- **Gateway/messages receiving module**. This module will receive the safety reports. It will be used via AS1 (email), AS2 (http/s), and AS3 (FTPs) protocols. There are different companies that provide out-of-the-shelf solutions for these modules.

Characteristic	Attribute	Description
Data Sensitivity	Type of Data	Sensitive and Personal Data
	Information Security and resilience	Information Security and resilience: High Integrity, High Confidentiality, High Availability
Scalability	New services required:	Yes, in the future
	Volatility of the demand	High for the external users and sources of reports, especially in cases of specific issue with a drug.
	Anticipated storage requirements for the next 5 years	Predictable, using current trend

	Peak of concurrent users	High, especially for reports in case of an issue with a drug being detected and made public.
	Proportion of Data in active use	High, as all the past data is used for the current reports.
Service Reliability, availability and performance requirements	Availability required	99.99% (High)
	Unplanned downtime	Less than 1 hour
	Real-time response	Medium
	Performance online	Standard reports are generated between agreed timelines based on 100 concurrent users.
	Performance batch	process at least 50000 safety reports per hour
Collaboration and Interoperatibilty	Possibility of retrofit information from searches (itself or search providers like Google trends)	Yes
	Possibility of integration with current health online systems like Google Health	Yes
Identity, authentication and access management	Identity Management	Identities of partners and users must be managed internally
	Credentials and permissions provisioning for users	Credentials of partners and users must be issued and managed internally, and must be verified before granting credentials.

	Role-Based Access Control (RBAC)	Yes
Encryption	Encryption	Yes during the transfer of the safety reports. It is recommended to encrypt the rest due to legal requirements
Legal and compliance	Data protection	Yes, applicable by law
	Access control	Both Mandatory access control and role based access control should be used.
	Accountability	Yes, by law
	Data location and legal jurisdiction	Yes, both by law

Table Table 18 - *List of characteristics and attributes of a pharmacovigilance implementation using cloud services*

The main module that is used here for testing of the framework is the gateway/messages-receiving module. The module will be implemented using an external provider company that host this functionality as a cloud service.

At this stage we need a set of attributes or characteristics that will be measured and chosen in order to decide which model will be implemented. In order to have more information about the requirements used in the framework for this pharmacovigilance module of the system we have used the ENISA (Catteddu Jan 2011) model. Table 1 shows some of the requirements that are used.

8.1.6   Benefits of the framework

The specified framework has a holistic approach, studying the system as a whole and taking into account as many parts of the system as required. It takes into account not only the internal parts of the system as other models do. A very important part of the framework is to take into account the interaction with the external cloud services and to analyse what could be the impact of these services in the complete system. This has been described especially in the first phase of the framework where both the internal view and the external view have been taken into account with the help of the monitoring authority.

This framework can be used for Micro Models (abstraction level is low/detail level is high), thus permitting the use of the framework for more detailed and specific scenarios. This has been provided as part of phase one and two, the analysis and the implementation of the MMD framework. As well, it can be used for Macro Models (abstraction is high/ detail level low), and combines both micro and macro models and be able to use them together to get better understanding of the systems, and be able to use more detailed data when there is the possibility. This is the case of the phases three and four. Where the data of the operational part of the system can be used. Especially the data of the services offered by external providers and the metrics of some of the attributes studied on these services by the monitoring authoritie.

The framework can be used in the operational phase of the system, permitting enhancements once the system is operational. In fact, phases one and two are used during the design and implementation phases respectively, but phases three and four are used during the operational phase of the MMD framework. It is very important, when using cloud services where the information is not known in advance, to use a framework that could provide information about the system during the operational phase.

The framework can get feedback from how it is working in real time to execute different actions automatically, providing a way to act directly into the system based on the information from current subsystems and cloud services. The possible use of automatic actions based on predefined rules allows the MMD framework to improve the way it works and adapt it to changes to the services provided by the external vendors.

Additionally, the framework supports multiple-source monitoring; getting information from different sources, some of them validated by authorities to obtain monitoring values that can be used for the calculation of the resilience and reliability values. Nevertheless, the aggregation rules need to be clearly defined for the monitoring if multiple sources will be used.

The proposed framework uses automatic Service Level Agreement (SLA) to obtain and check the SLA values. It allows to verify that the expected values are within the agreement or else to take automatic actions to solve the issue. The automatic SLA checking may be implemented using Web Level Service Agreements (WLSA) or other similar model for defining SLAs in an automatic way. In our framework most of the examples used are based on the WLSA defined by Patel (P. Patel 2009), but any other similar model could have been used.

8.1.7   Conclusions and future work

There are many risks in the utilisation of cloud computing in critical systems and most of them cannot be predicted in advance. This does not mean that cloud computing should not be used for critical systems, but it is necessary to determine the interrelations of these systems and the hidden risks before starting to use them. Until now SLAs and continuous service quality monitoring were the main tools for controlling risks. Similar techniques to those used for measuring the dependability of critical systems can be used, but more information regarding cloud computing risks and limitations must be added to these models to determine how cloud computing could affect those systems. We have introduced these risks and their consequences along with the concepts of micro- and macro-dependability.

Before cloud services are adopted by an organisation, especially for use in critical systems, interdependencies within the provider and within (and between) any other providers must be taken into account. Once the risks are clear, the right cloud service and model can be chosen. Whatever solution is chosen, there should be plans in case of cloud service unavailability and mechanisms should be in place to provide the service, even if a degraded one. In this way, our contribution provides a better understanding of the services that are like to be used in a cloud solution, showing the dependencies and how these affect the reliability of the services and can be improved trough cycles. The proposed framework has been mainly designed to be used on ICT systems and mainly cloud solutions. However, the model can be adapted for other type of systems and even for the interaction with non-ICT Systems. Also the roles of producers/consumers and supported/supporting Infrastructure with other CIs like the Electric grid.

"Computer science is no more about computers than astronomy is about telescopes."

[E. Dijkstra]

9 Appendix A: Pharmacovigilance

Before explain the requirements of the system I will try to introduce some concepts about pharmacovigilance (Mann and Andrews 2007). The purpose of pharmacovigilance (PhV) is the detection, assessment and prevention of adverse effects caused by medicines. The main purpose of pharmacovigilance is to minimize, in practice, the potential for harm that is associated with all active medicines. In order to do this currently governments all over the world collect safety reports of adverse drug reactions (ADR) from patients and healthcare providers using normally information systems. Once the reports are collected, are processed and evaluated normally using data mining tools in order to find hazards associated with medicines and prevent future harm to patients.

I have included some information about pharmacovigilance to give an understanding about what I will try to use as a model, I have tried to explain some basic concepts. For more information please refer to Patrick Waller (Waller n.d.) introduction to pharmacovigilance. (Mann and Andrews 2007)

Currently the WHO has the International Drug Monitoring Programme that provides pharmacovigilance for more than 100 countries. In the European Union the European Medicines Agency (EMA) is coordinating this; the system is called Eudravigilance, and is divided in two main databases for both human and veterinary medicines. In United States is mainly regulated by the FDA, but the pharmaceutical manufactures and some non-profit organizations are involved as well. In Japan the pharmacovigilance is regulated by the PMDA and the MHLW.

The main concepts related to pharmacovigilance that will be used in this work are:

- SAE: Serious Adverse event:

    - Death

    - Life-threatening

    - Requires hospitalization or prolongation of existing hospitalization

    - Persistent or significant disability or incapacity

    - Congenital anomaly

- Adverse events and Adverse reactions

    - An adverse event is any untoward event which happens in a patient in a clinical trial

    - An adverse reaction is one in which a causal association is suspected between the trial drug and the event

- Expected and unexpected adverse reactions

    - Not included (or more severe than) reactions listed in the applicable product information

- SUSAR: serious unexpected suspected adverse reaction

- SAR: serious adverse reaction

In order to help with harmonization of the information and to provide better cooperation between different pharmacovigilance systems standards like the ICH E2B are being created.

When creating a new drug, pharmaceutical companies are required by law in all countries to perform clinical trials of the new drug that are tested on people before they are approved. The manufacturers or their agents usually select a representative sample of patients for whom the drug is designed along with a comparable control group that may receive a placebo and/or another drug that is already marketed for the disease.

The main purpose of clinical trials is to discover if a drug works according to what is expected and how well the effect its, if it has any harmful effects, and its benefit-harm-risk profile, that basically says if it does do more good than harm, and how much more, and if it has a potential for harm, how probable and how serious is the harm? Sometimes the cons of the harm justify the benefits of the benefits for the patients.

Clinical trials in general, tell a lot of information about how well a drug works and what potential harm it may cause. They provide information which should be reliable for larger populations with the same characteristics as the trial group - age, gender, state of health, ethnic origin, and so on. The variables in a clinical trial are specified and controlled and the results relate only to the population of which the trial group is a representative sample. But a clinical trial can never tell the whole story of the effects of a drug in all situations. There are a lot of situations (like interactions with other drugs or foods) that will not occur until the drug is in the market. In order to control all these news cases that were not tested in the clinical trials the spontaneous reporting is used.

Once the drug is approved, the next stage is the post-marketing surveillance, and it is mainly based on spontaneous reporting is, relying on healthcare professionals (and sometimes consumers) to identify and report any suspected adverse drug reaction to their national pharmacovigilance centre or to the producer. Spontaneous reports are almost always submitted voluntarily. In many parts of the world these are submitted electronically using a defined message standard. All these type of reports are sent using a specific format, which has been defined and agreed, the template for the safety report safety message is shown in Figure 26 ICH M2 Safety Message   according to the Electronic Transmission of Individual Case Safety Reports Message Specification [CDER

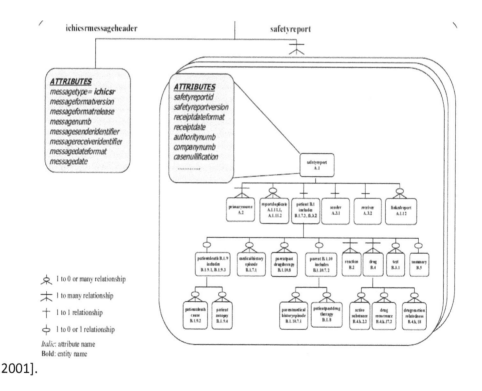

2001].

Figure 26 ICH M2 Safety Message (Center for Drug Evaluation and Research (CDER) Feb 2001)

Another problem is that in some cases overworked medical personnel do not report the reaction, mainly because they do not consider this a priority. Sometimes if the symptoms are not serious, they may not notice them at all. And even if the symptoms are serious, they may not be recognised as the effect of a particular drug.

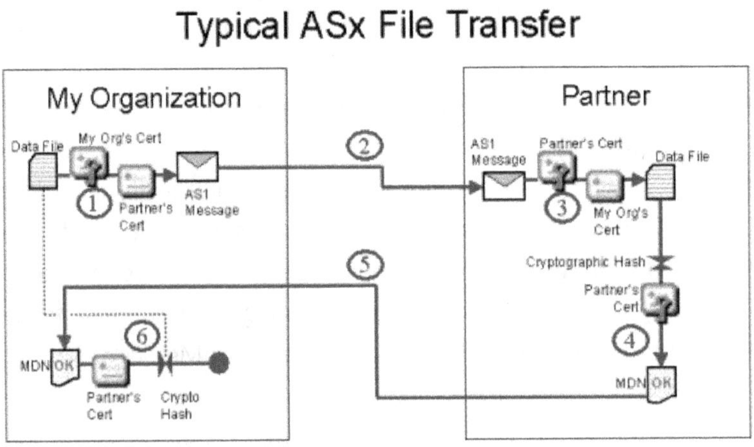

Typical ASx File Transfer

Figure 27 Typical implementation of ASx file transfer by company IPSwitch

- **Messages Processing / business rules module**
  - o The message processing module will implement the main business rules for treating the safety reports, as well as the more complex validation rules, some basic validation rules will be implemented in the Gateway/message module. Figure 27 Typical implementation of ASx file transfer by company IPSwitch.
  - o Message duplication detection will be done in this module as well.
- **Web access**
  - o The system will implement a web access mechanism to provide access to all the functionality
  - o This module will be used as the main portal and access tool to the rest of the modules.
- **Reporting module**
  - o This module will permit run preformatted reports that are created by the scientific administrators, it will be used by the general public and healthcare professionals
- **Security module**

     o Will apply the security, there are different options, from username/password to certificates or physical devices.

- **Datawarehouse/data mining module**
  - One of the main modules, that will permit to a small number of scientific users create specific reports or use data mining tools. Usually these modules will be implemented using current tools in the markets.

10 Bibliography

(EUC), E. U. (2009). *Protecting Europe against large-scale cyber attacks* (Vol. October). (". o. Lords", Ed.) 5th Report of Session.

[USTUTT-HLRS], E. G., & Editors: Keith Jeff ery [ERCIM], B. N.-L. (2009). *The Future of Cloud Computing.* Brussels: European Commission: Information Society and Media.

A. Bondavalli, I. M. (1999). Automatic dependability analysis for supporting design decisions in UML. *4th IEEE International Symposium on High Assurance Systems Engineering.*

Abbadi, I. (2011). Operational trust in Clouds' environment. *Computers and Communications (ISCC), 2011 IEEE Symposium on* (pp. 141-145). Kerkyra: IEEE.

Ahrens, M. (2010). Cloud computing and the impact on enterprise IT. *FIS'10 Proceedings of the Third future internet conference on Future internet* (pp. 148-155). Springer-Verlag .

Alexander Keller, H. L. (2002). The WSLA Framework: Specifying and Monitoring Service Level Agreements for Web Services. *JOURNAL OF NETWORK AND SYSTEMS MANAGEMENT, 11*(1), 57-81.

Alhamad, M., Dillon, T., & Chang, E. (2010). Conceptual SLA framework for cloud computing. *Digital Ecosystems and Technologies (DEST), 2010 4th IEEE International Conference on* (pp. 606 - 610). Perth, Australia: IEEE.

Andrieux, A., Czajkowski, K., Dan, A., Keahey, K., Ludwig, H., Nakata, T., et al. (2007). *Web Services Agreement Specification.* Retrieved from Open Grid Forum: http://www.ogf.org/documents/GFD.107.pdf

Armbrust, I, S., M, Z., A, F., R, G., AD, J., et al. (2010, April). A view of cloud computing. *Comunications of the ACM*, 50-58.

Avizienis, A., Laprie, J.-C., Randell, B., & Landwehr, C. (2004). Basic Concepts and Taxonomy of Dependable and Secure Computing. *IEEE Transactions on Dependable and Secure Computing, 1*, 11-33.

Bastani, C. V. (1982, July). Software reliability: Status and perspectives. *IEEE Trans. Software Eng., SE-8*, 59- 371.

Berkeley, A. R., & Wallace, M. (2010). *A Framework for Establishing Critical Infrastructure Resilience Goals.* National Infrastructure Advisory Council, Final Report and Recommendations by the Council. National Infrastructure Advisory Council.

Bertolucci, J. (2012, 10 23). Why We Need To Mine Government's Big Data. *Informationweek.*

Borras, J., Webbe, D., Mattocks, C., & Aanesen, H. A. (2013, March 19). *The future service model for home and community health care.* (EPRForum, Ed.) Retrieved September 4, 2013, from OASIS E-Health: https://www.oasis-open.org/committees/document.php?document_id=48583&wg_abbrev=bcm

Bouchon, S. (2006). The vulnerability of interdependent critical infrastructures systems: epistemological and conceptual state-of-the-art. (J. R. Centre, Ed.) *EU Report.*

Boudali, H., Haverkort, B. R., Kuntz, M., & Stoelinga, M. (2007). Best of Three Worlds: Towards Sound Architectural Dependability Models. *8th International Workshop on Performability Modeling of Computer and Communication Systems (PMCCS).* Edinburgh, UK.

Bourgeau, T., Chaouchi, H., & Kirci, P. (2013). Machine-to-Machine Communications. *Computer Communications and Networks*, 221-241.

Calheiros, R. N. (2011). CloudSim: a toolkit for modeling and simulation of cloud computing environments and evaluation of resource provisioning algorithms. *Software: Practice and Experience,*(41), 23-50.

Canada Cloud Strategy. (n.d.). Retrieved from Canada Cloud Strategy: http://www.scribd.com/doc/20818613/Cloud-Computing-and-the-Canadian-Environment

Cao, J. J. (2002). ARMS: An agent-based resource management system for grid computing. *Scientific Programming, 10*, 135-148.

Catteddu, D. (Jan 2011). *Security & Resilience in Governmental Clouds. Making an informed decision.* European Network and Information Security Agency.

Center for Drug Evaluation and Research (CDER). (Feb 2001). *Electronic Transmission of Individual Case Safety Reports Message Specification. ICH ICSR DTD Version 2.1.* U.S. Food and Drug Administration.

Chang, Y.-K. L.-C. (2012, January 26). *Patent No. 12/926,468.* US.

Chen, W. Z. (2010). From E-government to C-government via Cloud Computing. *E-Business and E-Government (ICEE), 2010 International Conference on* (pp. 679 - 682). Guangzhou : IEEE.

Christopher A. Cannin, B. W. (2009). Trends in Information Security Regulation. In C.-T. Li, *Handbook of Research on Computational Forensics, Digital Crime, and Investigation: Methods and Solutions.* Warwick, UK: Information Science Reference.

Cloud Security Alliance. (2011). *Security Guidance for Critical areas of cloud computing v3.0.* Retrieved from Cloud Security Alliance Security Guidance: https://cloudsecurityalliance.org/guidance/csaguide.v3.0.pdf

Commerce, U. D. (n.d.). *U.S.-EU & U.S.-Swiss Safe Harbor Frameworks*. Retrieved from export.gov: http://export.gov/safeharbor/

Commerce, US Deparment of. (2010). *U.S.-EU & U.S.-Swiss Safe Harbor Frameworks*. Retrieved from export.gov: http://export.gov/safeharbor/

computer security division, N. (2011). *FISMA Detailed Overview*. (N. I. Technology, Producer) Retrieved from FISMA: http://csrc.nist.gov/groups/SMA/fisma/overview.html

computer security division, N. (n.d.). *FISMA Detailed Overview*. (N. I. Technology, Producer) Retrieved from FISMA: http://csrc.nist.gov/groups/SMA/fisma/overview.html

CSA. (2009). *Security & Resilience in Governmental Clouds.* Security Guidance for Critical Areas of Focus in Cloud Computing V2.1: Cloud Security Alliance.

CSA. (2010). *CSA Top Threats to cloud computing v1.0.* Cloud Security Alliance.

CSA. (2011). *CSA Cloud controls Matrix V1.1.* Cloud Security Alliance.

Dai, Y. X. (2003). A study of service reliability and availability for distributed systems. *Reliability Engineering & System Safety, 79*, 103-112.

Daniel Nurmi, R. W. (2009). *The eucalyptus Open-Source Clod-computing system.* Santa Barbara, California, USA: Computer Science Departement, University of California.

Deming, W. E. (1986). *Out of the Crisis.* (M. I. Technology, Ed.) MIT Center for Advanced Engineering Study.

Dhillon, B. (2003). Engineering Safety. *Series on Industrial & Systems Engineering. Wold Scientific, 1.*

Diez O, S. A. (2011). Reliability issues related to the usage of cloud computing in critical infrastructures. *ESREL 2011* (p. 414). Troyes: European Safety and Reliability Associationability Association).

Diez, O., & Silva, A. (2013). Govcloud: Using Cloud Computing in Public Organizations. *IEEE Technol. Soc. Mag. , 32*(1), 66-72.

Egan, M. J. (2007). Anticipating Future Vulnerability: Defining Characteristics of Incresingly Critical Infrastruc-true-like Systems. *Journal of Contingencies and Crisis Management, 15*(1), pp. pp 4-17.

European Medecines Agency (EMA). (2011, 10). *About EUTCT.* Retrieved 08 2013, from
http://eutct.ema.europa.eu/eutct/jsp/common/eutct_about.html#toc0

Fahmy, H. (2001). Reliability evaluation in distributed computing environments using the AHP. *Computer Networks,, 36*, 597-615.

Foster, I. K. (2002). Grid services for distributed system integration. *Computer, 35*, 37-46.

Fu, S. (2011). Performance Metric Selection for Autonomic Anomaly Detection on Cloud Computing Systems. *Global Telecommunications Conference (GLOBECOM 2011), 2011 IEEE* (pp. 1-5). IEEE.

G. Dummer, R. W. (1997). *An Elementray Guide to Reliability* (Vol. July). Butterworth-Heinemann.

Garlick, G. (2011). Improving Resilience with Community Cloud Computing. *Sixth International Conference on Availability, Reliability and Security* (pp. 650 - 655). Vienna: IEEE.

Gary Marshall, D. C. (2002). *Resilience, Reliability and Redundancy.* Copper Development Association, IEE. Brussels: Copper Development Association.

Gerard Briscoe, A. M. (2009). *Digital Ecosystems in the Clouds: Towards Community Cloud Computing.* New York: 3rd IEEE International Conference on Digital Ecosystems and Technologies.

Gewndal Le Grand, M. R. (2004). A global framework to enhance critical infrastructure protection. *Securing Critical Infrastructures.* Grenoble.

Giannakaki, M. (2011). *EU Data Protection Directive revised New challenges and perspectives.* Athens: KARAGEORGIOU.

Goel, A. L. (1985, 12). Software reliability models: Assumptions, Limitations and Applycability. *IEEE Transactions on Software engineering , SE-11*(12), 1411-1423.

Goel, Amrit L.; Okumoto, Kazu. (1979, August). Time-Dependent Error-Detection Rate Model for Software Reliability and Other Performance Measures. *Reliability, IEEE Transactions on, 28*(3), 206 - 211.

Goldston, D. (2008, 9 4). Data wrangling. *Nature, 455*(7209).

Government, U. (2012). *data.gov.uk.* Retrieved from data.gov.uk: http://data.gov.uk

group, O. g. (2007, December 8). *8 Principles of Open Government Data.* Retrieved August 28, 2013, from Open Government Data: http://www.opengovdata.org/home/8principles

Gustavsson, R., & Stå hl, B. (2010). The empowered user - The critical interface to critical infrastructures. *Critical Infrastructure (CRIS), 2010 5th International Conference on* (pp. 1-3). IEEE.

Hogben, D. C. (Nov 2009). *Cloud Computing: Benefits, risks and recommendations for information Security.* European Network and Information Security Agency.

Horowitz, B. T. (2012, 3 26). IBM Watson to Aid Sloan-Kettering With Cancer Research. *eWeek*.

Humbetov, S. (2012). Data-intensive computing with map-reduce and hadoop. *Application of Information and Communication Technologies (AICT), 2012 6th International Conference on* (pp. 1-5). Tbilisi, Georgia: IEEE.

IBM. (2011, Feb). *BM and FONAFE Bring Cloud Computing to Critical Government Services in Peru.* Retrieved from http://www-03.ibm.com/press/us/en/pressrelease/33810.wss

IBM. (n.d.). *Hospital for Sick Children Leveraging key data to provide proactive patient care.* IBM. IBM.

IBM Software. (2012, May). *TerraEchos: Streaming data technology supports covert intelligence and surveillance sensor systems.* Retrieved August 2013, from http://public.dhe.ibm.com/common/ssi/ecm/en/imc14726usen/IMC14726USEN.PDF

IEC. (n.d.). *Dependability and quality of service* . Retrieved from IEC: http://dom2.iec.ch/iev/iev.nsf/display?openform&ievref=191-02-03

IFIP WG10.4 on Dependable computing and Fault Tolerance . (n.d.). Retrieved from Dependability: http://www.dependability.org/

International Conference on Harmonisation of Technical Requirements for Registration of Pharmaceuticals for Human Use (ICH). (2013). *MedDRA.* Retrieved 2013, from http://www.ich.org/products/meddra.html

Isard, M., Budiu, M., Yu, Y., Birrell, A., & Fetterly, D. (2007). Dryad: distributed data-parallel programs from sequential building blocks. *Proceedings of the 2nd ACM SIGOPS/EuroSys European Conference on Computer Systems.* New York.

Jeffery, K. N.-L. (2009). *The Future of Cloud Computing, Opportunities for European Cloud Computing Beyond 2010.* European Commission, Information Society and Media. Cordis.

JiSu Park, H. Y. (2011). Markov Chain based Monitoring Service for Fault Tolerance in Mobile Cloud Computing. *Advanced Information Networking and Applications (WAINA),* (pp. 520 - 525). Biopolis: IEEE.

Joshi, K., Bunker, G., Jahanian, F., van Moorsel, A., & Weinman, J. (2009). Dependability in the Cloud: Challenges and Opportunities. . *International Conference on Dependable Systems & Networks.* IEEE/IFIP .

Kasumigaseki Japan Cloud Strategy. (n.d.). Retrieved from Kasumigaseki Japan Cloud Strategy: http://www.cloudbook.net/directories/gov-clouds/gov-program.php?id=100016

Kenneth P. Birman, L. G. (2011). Running Smart Grid Control Software on Cloud Computing Architectures. *Workshop on Computational Needs for the Next Generation Electric Grid.* NY: Cornell University.

Kevin L. Jackson, R. W. (2011). *The Economic Benefit of Cloud Computing .* NJVC and Clear Government Solutions.

Kroeker, K. L. (2009, March). The evolution of virtualization. *Communications of the ACM - Being Human in the Digital Age, 52*(3), 18-20.

Kröger, W., & Zio, E. (2011). *Vulnerable Systems.* London: Springer.

Kumar, A. a. (1996). Parameters for system effectiveness evaluation of distributed systems. *IEEE Transactions on Computers, 45*, 746-752.

Kumar, V. H. (1986, 12). Distributed program reliability analysis. *IEEE Transactions on Software Engineering*, 42-50.

Kundra, V. (2010). *State of Public Sector Cloud Computing .* CIO.gov, CIO Council. CIO Council.

L., B. (2011, July 1). *Cloud Computing Efficiency.* Retrieved from Applied Clinical Trials: http://www.appliedclinicaltrialsonline.com/appliedclinicaltrials/article/articleDetail.jsp?id=730574

Laprie, J., & LAAS-CNRS. (n.d.). Resilience for the scalability of dependability. *Network Computing and Applications, Fourth IEEE International Symposium* (pp. 5-6). Cambridge,MA: IEEE.

Lavenue, J.-J. (2009). *L'E-sécurité au risque de l'externalisation dans la société numérisée* (Vol. October). Université de Lille.

Lentz, R. F. (2009, May). *U.S. House of Representatives Armed Services committee of terrorism, unconventional threats & capabilities.* Retrieved from http://armedservices.house.gov/pdfs/TUTC050509/Lentz_Testimony0505 09.pdf

Lewis, T. G. (2006). *Critical Infrastructure Protection in Homeland Security. Defending a networked nation.* Wiley-Interscience.

Linhares, M., de Oliveira, R., Farines, J.-M., & Vernadat, F. (2007). Introducing the modeling and verification process in SysML. *Emerging Technologies and Factory Automation, 2007. ETFA. IEEE Conference on* (pp. 344 - 351). Patras: IEEE.

Lipowicz, A. (2009, April). *Cloud computing moves into public safety.* Retrieved from Federal computer week: http://fcw.com/articles/2009/04/16/cloud-computing-moving-into-public-safety-realm.aspx

Lipowicz, A. (2009, April 16). *Cloud computing moves into public safety.* Retrieved from   Federalcomputerweek   : http://www.pscr.gov/about_pscr/press/voip/cloud_computing_moves_in to_public_safety_042009-federal_computer_week.pdf

M, A., I, S., M, Z., A, F., R, G., AD, J., et al. (2010, April). A view of cloud computing. *Comunications of the ACM*, 50-58.

M. Xie, Y. D. (2004). *Computing System Reliability: Models and Analysis.* Springer.

Machanavajjhala, A., & Reiter, J. P. (2012). Big privacy: protecting confidentiality in big data. *XRDS, 19*(1), 20-23.

Madden, S. (2012). From Databases to Big Data. *Internet Computing, 16*(3), 4-6.

Madni, A. (2009, June). Towards a Conceptual Framework for Resilience Engineering. *Systems Journal, 3*(2), 181-191.

Malek, M. (2008). Online Dependability Assessment through Runtime Monitoring and Prediction. *Dependable Computing Conference, 2008. EDCC 2008. Seventh European* (p. 181). Kaunas: IEEE.

Malhotra, M. (1995, Sept). Dependability modeling using Petri-nets. *Reliability, IEEE Transactions on, 44*(3), 428 - 440 .

Mann, R. D., & Andrews, E. B. (2007). *Pharmacovigilance. Second Edition.* John Wiley & Son.

Marc Mercuri, U. H. (2012, 11 1). *Failsafe: Guidance for Resilient Cloud Architectures.* Retrieved 12 12, 2013, from Windows Azure: http://msdn.microsoft.com/en-us/library/windowsazure/jj853352.aspx

Mark Shumbera, R. D. (2012). *DNA Sequence Analysis Solution for Identification of Aptamer Candidates.* TechAmerica Foundation, TechAmerica Foundation. Washington: Federal Big Data Commission.

Martin Bellamy, G. G. (2011). *DATA CENTRE STRATEGY, G-CLOUD & GOVERNMENT APPLICATIONS STORE PROGRAMME PHASE 2 SCOPE REPORT .* UK Cabinet Office. UK Cabinet Office.

Mehine, J. (2011). *Large Scale Data Analysis Using Apache Pig.* Tartu: Institute of Computer Science, FACULTY OF MATHEMATICS AND COMPUTER SCIENCE, UNIVERSITY OF TARTU.

Mena, L. J., Felix, V. G., Ostos, R., Gonzalez, J. A., Cervantes, A., Ochoa, A., et al. (2013). Mobile Personal Health System for Ambulatory Blood Pressure Monitoring. *Computational and Mathematical Methods in Medicine, 2013*(doi:10.1155/2013/598196), 13.

Michael Armbrust, A. F. (Feb 2009). *Above the Clouds: A Berkeley view of cloud computing.* University of California at Berkeley: Electrical Engineering and Computer Sciences.

Microsoft. (2013). *Introduction to Windows Azure HDInsight Service.* (Microsoft) Retrieved 2013, from http://www.windowsazure.com/en-us/manage/services/hdinsight/introduction-hdinsight/

Miller, R. (2009, April 3). *FBI Seizes Servers at Dallas Data Center.* Retrieved from Datacenter knowledge: http://www.datacenterknowledge.com/archives/2009/04/03/fbi-seizes-servers-at-dallas-data-center/

Mills., H. D. (1972). *On the statistical validation of computer programs.* IBM Federal Syst. Div. Gaithersburg: IBM.

Moranda, P. B. (1975). Prediction of software reliability during debugging. *Reliability and Maintainability*, (pp. 327-332). Washington.

Moranda, Z. J. (1972). Software reliability research. In *In Statistical Computer Performance Evaluation* (pp. 465-484). New York: W. Freiberger.

Moteff, J., & Parfomak, P. (October 2004). *Critical Infrastructure and Key Assets: Definition and Identification.* Report for Congress.

Musa, J. D. (1971). A theory of software reliability and its application. *IEEE Trans. Software Eng*, 312-327.

Mutavdzi, R. (2010). Cloud Computing Architectures for National, Regional and Local Government. *MIPRO, 2010 Proceedings of the 33rd International Convention. 24-28*, pp. 1322 - 1327. Opatija, Croatia: IEEE.

Nelson, E. (1978). Estimating software reliability from test data. *Microelectron. Rel., 17*, 67-74.

Okumoto, A. L. (1978). An analysis of recurrent software failures in a real-time control system. *Proc. ACM Annu. Tech. Conf* (pp. 496-500). Washington: IEEE.

Olavsrud, T. (2012, 8 1). U.S. Agencies Struggling to Crack Big Data. *CIO, 25*(15).

Oracle. (2011). *Oracle Argus Safety.* Retrieved from http://www.oracle.com/us/industries/health-sciences/027630.htm

P. Patel, A. R. (2009). Service Level Agreement in Cloud Computing. *Cloud Workshops at OOPSLA09.*

Pan, J. (1999). *Software Reliability.* Retrieved from Dependable Embebbed Systems Carnegie Mellon University: http://www.ece.cmu.edu/~koopman/des_s99/sw_reliability/

Park, M. P. (2009). Cloud Computing: Future solution for e-Governance. *ICEGOV '09 Proceedings of the 3rd international conference on Theory and practice of electronic governance.* ACM.

Perrow, C. (1999). *Normal Accidents.* Princeton University Press.

Pierre, S. a. (1990). An artificial intelligence approach for improving computer communications network topologies. *ournal of Operational Research Society, 41*(5), 405-418.

Pietrantuono, R., Russo, S., & Trivedi, K. (2010). Online monitoring of software system reliability. *Dependable Computing Conference (EDCC)* (pp. 209-218). IEEE.

Poh, M. X.-S.-L. (2004). *Computing System Reliability Models and Analysis.* Singapore: KLUWER ACADEMIC PUBLISHERS.

Policy, O. o. (2012, 3 29). *OBAMA ADMINISTRATION "BIG DATA" INITIATIVE.* Executive Office of the President . Washington: Office of Science and Technology Policy Executive Office of the President.

Rahul Ghosh, K. S. (2010). *Interacting Markov Chain Based Hierarchical Approach for Cloud Services.* IBM Research Division, Department of ECE Duke University . Durham: IBM Research.

Rajkumar Buyyaa, C. S. (2009, June). Cloudcomputing and emerging IT platforms: Vision, hype, and reality for delivering computing as the 5thutility. *Future Generation Computer Systems, 25*(6), 599-616 .

Ranganathan, P., & Chang, J. (2012, Jan-Feb). (Re)Designing Data-Centric Data Centers. *Micro, 32*(1), 66-70.

Rinaldi, S. M. (2004). Modeling and Simulating Critical Infrastructures and Their Interdependencies. *Hawaii International Conference on Systems Sciences.* Sandia Nat. Labs., Albuquerque, NM, USA: IEEE.

Rinaldi, S., Peerenboom, J., & Kelly, T. (2001). *Identifying, understanding, and analyzing critical infrastructure inter-dependencies.* Washington, DC: Air Force Quadrennial Defense Review.

Risk Steering Committee. Department of Homeland Security. (2010). *DHS Risk Lexicon.* USA: . Department of Homeland Security.

Robinson, S., & Higton, N. (2007, MARCH 20). Computer simulation for quality and reliability engineering. *Quality and Reliability Engineering International, 11*(5), 371–377.

Shackelford, K. (2011, July 29). *NASA Nebula project.* Retrieved from nasa.gov: http://nebula.nasa.gov

Shooman, M. L. (1972). Probabilistic models for software reliability prediction. *Statistical Computer Performance Evaluation*, 485-502.

staff, D. I. (2010, 5 10). Retrieved from Defense Industry Daily : http://www.defenseindustrydaily.com/defense-cloud-computing-06387/

Sterbenz, J. P., Hutchison, D., Cetinkaya, E. K., Jabbar, A., Rohrer, J. P., Sholler, M., et al. (2010). Resilience and survivability in communication networks: Strategies, principles, and survey of disciplines. *Computer Network 54.*

Steven A. Mills, S. L. (2012). *Demystifying Big Data: A Practical Guide To Transforming The Business Of Government.* TechAmerica Foundation, Federal Big Data Commission. Washington: TechAmerica.

Stewart Baker, S. &. (2010). *In the Crossfire: Critical Infrastructure in the Age of Cyber War.* London: McAfee International Ltd.

Sun, D., Chang, G., Guo, Q., Wang, C., & Wang, X. (2010). A Dependability Model to Enhance Security of Cloud Environment Using System-Level Virtualization Techniques. *Pervasive Computing Signal Processing and Applications (PCSPA), 2010 First International Conference on* (pp. 305-310). IEEE.

Sundmaeker, H., Guillemin, P., Friess, P., & Woelfflé, S. (2010). *Vision and Challenges for Realising the Internet of Things.* Brussels: European Commission - Information Society and Media DG.

technology, N. G. (2001). *Safeware. System Safety and Computers.* Addison-Wesley.

Tomasz Wiktor Wlodarczyk, C. R.-I. (2009). Industrial Cloud: Toward Inter-enterprise Inte-gration. *CloudCom 2009.* Beijing: Springer .

Trivedi, K. S., Kim, D. S., & Ghosh, R. (2009). Resilience in Computer Systems and
Networks. *Proceedings of the 2009 International Conference on
Computer-Aided Design.* ACM.

Troger, P. (2011, 11 17). Dependability in Cloud Computing. Germany.

UK Government Cloud Strategy. (n.d.). Retrieved from UK G Cloud strategy:
http://www.cabinetoffice.gov.uk/sites/default/files/resources/governme
nt-cloud-strategy_0.pdf

Undheim, A., Chilwan, A., & Heegaard, P. (2011). Differentiated Availability in
Cloud Computing SLAs. (pp. 129 - 136). Lyon: IEEE.

Use, I. C. (2001, February). *ICH HARMONISED TRIPARTITE GUIDELINE .* Retrieved
from MAINTENANCE OF THE ICH GUIDELINE ON CLINICAL SAFETY DATA
MANAGEMENT : DATA ELEMENTS FOR TRANSMISSION OF INDIVIDUAL
CASE   SAFETY   REPORTS   E2B(R2)   :
http://www.ich.org/fileadmin/Public_Web_Site/ICH_Products/Guidelines
/Efficacy/E2B/Step4/E2B_R2__Guideline.pdf

Vacca, J. R. (2004). *Public Key Infrastructure: Building Trusted Applications and
Web Services.* Auerbach Publications.

Vangelova, L. (2012, 9). Data Scientist. *The Science Teacher, 79*(6), 66-67.

Vincenzo Fioriti, G. D. (2010). On Modeling and Measuring Inter-dependencies
among Critical Infrastructures. *Complexity in Engineering*, IEEE.

Vouk, M. A. (2008). Cloud Computing – Issues, Research and Implementations.
Journal of Computing and Information Technology, 235-246.

Waller, P. (n.d.). *An introduction to pharmacovigilance.* 2010: Wiley-Blackwell.

Wang, K. X. (2008). Cooperative Monitoring for Internet Data Centers.
*Performance, Computing and Communications Conference, 2008. IPCCC
2008.* (pp. 111-118). IEEE International .

Weibull. (2010). *The Reliability Function.* Retrieved from Reliability Engineering
Resources:
http://www.weibull.com/AccelTestWeb/the_reliability_function.htm

Wolverton, G. J. (1973). Assessment of software reliability. *11th Annu. Meeting German Oper. Res. Soc., DGOR, Hamburg, Germany; also in Proc. Oper. Res* (pp. 395-422). Physica-Verlag, Wirzberg-Wien.

Yeh, W. (2003). An evaluation of the multi-state node networks reliability using the traditional binary-state networks reliability algorithm. *Reliability Engineering & System Safety, 81*, 1-7.

Yiu, C. (2012). *The Big Data Opportunity.* Policy Exchange, London.

Yuan-Shun Dai, B. Y. (2010). *Cloud Service Reliability: Modeling and Analysis.* National Science Foundatio.

Zeitler, D. (1991). Realistic assumptions for software reliability models. *Software Reliability Engineering, 1991. Proceedings., 1991 International Symposium on* (pp. 67 - 74). Austin, TX , USA : IEEE.

Zhang, L.-J. (2007). SOA Solution Reference Architecture. *Web Services, 2007. ICWS 2007* (p. xxxvi). Salt Lake City, UT, USA: IEEE.

Zhang, L.-J. (2012). Big Services Era: Global Trends of Cloud Computing and Big Data. *Services Computing, IEEE Transactions on , 5*(4), 467 - 468.

11 Figures

12 Tables & Equations

```
#define TRUE FALSE //Happy debugging
//END
```

www.ingramcontent.com/pod-product-compliance
Lightning Source LLC
Chambersburg PA
CBHW080404060326
40689CB00019B/4124